Teach Yourself®

Get started in Italian

Vittoria Bowles

Advisory editor
Paul Coggle

Revised by
Nick J Broom

The publisher has used its best endeavours to ensure that the URLs
for external websites referred to in this book are correct and active
at the time of going to press. However, the publisher and the author
have no responsibility for the websites and can make no guarantee
that a site will remain live or that the content will remain relevant,
decent or appropriate.

For UK order enquiries: please contact Bookpoint Ltd,
130 Milton Park, Abingdon, Oxon OX14 4SB.
Telephone: +44 (0) 1235 827720. Fax: +44 (0) 1235 400454. Lines are
open 09.00–17.00, Monday to Saturday, with a 24-hour message
answering service. Details about our titles and how to order are
available at www.teachyourself.co.uk

For USA order enquiries: please contact McGraw-Hill Customer
Services, PO Box 545, Blacklick OH 43004-0545, USA.
Telephone: 1-800-722-4726. Fax: 1-614-755-5645.

For Canada order enquiries: please contact McGraw-Hill Ryerson Ltd, 300
Water St, Whitby, Ontario L1N 9B6, Canada. Telephone: 905 430 5000.
Fax: 905 430 5020.

Long renowned as the authoritative source for self-guided learning –
with more than 50 million copies sold worldwide – the Teach Yourself
series includes over 500 titles in the fields of languages, crafts,
hobbies, business, computing and education.

British Library Cataloguing in Publication Data: a catalogue record
for this title is available from the British Library.

Library of Congress Catalog Card Number: on file.

First published in UK 1992 as Teach Yourself Beginner's Italian by
Hodder Education, part of Hachette Livre UK, 338 Euston Road,
London NW1 3BH.

First published in US 1992 as Teach Yourself Beginner's Italian by
The McGraw-Hill Companies, Inc.

This edition published 2012.

The Teach Yourself name is a registered trade mark of Hodder
Headline.

Illustrated by Barking Dog Art, Sally Elford, Peter Lubach

Typeset by Integra Software Services Pvt. Ltd., Pondicherry, India

Printed by Ashford Colour Press Ltd

Hachette Livre UK's policy is to use papers that are natural,
renewable and recyclable products and made from wood grown in
sustainable forests. The logging and manufacturing processes are
expected to conform to the environmental regulations of the country
of origin.

Impression number	10 9 8 7 6
Year	2019

Contents

Meet the author

I married my English husband in 1973 and left my home town in Liguria to come and live on the south coast of England. Almost immediately, I was asked by the local council to take some Italian classes. My students were mostly older than me (musicians, lecturers, the odd retired colonel), and their love for my country helped me greatly to settle here. As their conversations and 'presentations' gained in fluency and accuracy, I was learning a great deal about England and, above all, its people. Many of my pupils invited my husband and me to their glorious Sunday dinners, and we had them visiting us to sample my home-made ravioli and other Italian dishes. I soon started to travel further afield in the area, with more and more classes, until the then Brighton Polytechnic (now University of Brighton) asked me to develop and teach some intensive summer residential courses for their staff and other courses such as those for airline, bank and medical staff.

One of the most challenging tasks (which I undertook for about 15 years) was that of developing and teaching an intensive Italian course for students attending the BSc European Management with Technology (sponsored by the European Student Exchange Programme, supported by the European Commission): each year, 30 university students with no knowledge of Italian had to spend their second term in Italy, while their Italian colleagues came to England.

During the first term, the 'freshers', as well as following five other subjects, had to learn sufficient Italian to be able to survive in Italy, to understand lectures on subjects such as business management and technology, take notes and pass their examinations, all in Italian – a tour de force they managed remarkably well, proving wrong those who thought it was an impossible task. In fact, the course was awarded the Unilever prize for Innovation. I hope you will enjoy your studies of Italian with me as your guide.

Vittoria Bowles

Credits

How the course works

This course is divided into two parts: the first has **ten units**, the second has **eight**. The first part deals with what are termed language *functions*, that is, each unit covers particular principles of the language that are common to many different situations. It is important that you tackle the first ten units **thoroughly** and in the order in which they are presented. Practise them until they become second nature and only then proceed to the second part of the book. To help you practise, there is a **review unit** after the **third**, **sixth** and **tenth** units.

The units in the second part expand on and better illustrate the points made in the first, in addition to introducing further topics. These units may be studied in whatever sequence you prefer.

On the following pages there is also a **study skills** section, **Learn to learn**, which is designed to enable you to get the very best out of this course. There are also guides to **pronunciation** and **useful expressions** in Italian.

To make your learning easier and more efficient, a system of icons indicates the actions you should take:

 Play the audio track

 New words and phrases

 Figure something out for yourself

 Culture tip

 Exercises coming up!

 Reading exercise

 Writing practice

 Speaking practice

 Check your Italian ability (no cheating)

A FEW WORDS ABOUT THE AUDIO

While you are working with the book, start by listening to the audio and try to understand what is being said. Go over each dialogue bit by bit with the assistance of the **Vocabulary builder** until you are confident that you understand every word; pause and replay the recording when needed.

Learn to learn: be successful at learning languages

The Discovery Method – learn to learn!

There are lots of philosophies and approaches to language learning, some practical, some quite unconventional, and far too many to list here. Perhaps you know of a few, or even have some techniques of your own. In this book we have incorporated the **Discovery Method** of learning, a sort of DIY approach to language learning. What this means is that you will be encouraged throughout the course to engage your mind and work out the language for yourself, through identifying patterns, understanding grammar concepts, noticing words that are similar to English, and more. This method promotes *language awareness*, a critical skill in acquiring a new language. As a result of your own efforts, you will be able to better retain what you have learned, use it with confidence and, even better, apply those same skills to *continuing* to learn the language (or, indeed, another one) on your own after you've finished this book.

Everyone can succeed in learning a language – the key is to know *how* to learn it. Learning is more than just reading or memorizing grammar and vocabulary. It's about being an *active* learner, learning in real contexts, and, most importantly, *using* what you've learned in different situations. Simply put, if you **work something out for yourself**, you're more likely to understand it. And when you use what you've learned, you're more likely to remember it.

And because many of the essential but (let's admit it!) dull details, such as grammar rules, are introduced through the **Discovery Method**, you'll have more fun while learning. Soon, the language will start to make sense and you'll be relying on your own intuition to construct original sentences *independently*, not just listening and repeating.

Enjoy yourself!

1 Make a habit out of learning

Study a little every day, between 20 and 30 minutes if possible, rather than two to three hours in one session. **Give yourself short-term goals**, e.g. work out how long you'll spend on a particular unit and work within the time limit. This will help you to **create a study habit**, much in the same way you would in a sport or in music. You will need to concentrate, so try to **create an environment conducive to learning**, which is calm and quiet and free from distractions. As you study, do not worry about your mistakes or the things you can't remember or understand. Languages settle differently in our brains, but gradually the language will become clearer as your brain starts to make new connections. Just **give yourself enough time** and you will succeed.

2 Expand your language contact

As part of your study habit try to take other opportunities to **expose yourself to the language**. As well as using this book you could try listening to radio and television or reading articles and blogs. Perhaps you could find information in Italian about a personal passion or hobby or even a news story that interests you. In time you'll find that your vocabulary and language recognition deepen and you'll become used to a range of writing and speaking styles.

3 Vocabulary

▶ To organize your study of vocabulary, group new words under:

    a   **generic categories, e.g.** *food, furniture*

    b   **situations in which they occur, e.g. under** *restaurant* **you can write** *waiter, table, menu, bill*

    c   **functions, e.g.** *greetings, parting, thanks, apologizing.*

▶ Say the words out loud as you read them.
▶ Write the words over and over again. Remember that if you want to keep lists on your smartphone or tablet you can usually switch the keyboard language to make sure you are able to include all accents and special characters.
▶ Listen to the audio several times.
▶ You will often notice missing words in the Vocabulary builder. Look for patterns to help you complete the lists.

- ▶ Cover up the English side of the vocabulary list and see if you remember the meaning of the word.
- ▶ Associate the words with similar sounding words in English, e.g. **parlare** (*to speak*) with *parlour*, a room where people chat.
- ▶ Create flash cards, drawings and mind maps.
- ▶ Write out words for objects you have in your house and stick them to the objects.
- ▶ Pay attention to patterns in words, e.g. adding **buon** or **buona** to the start of a word usually indicates a greeting: **buongiorno**, **buonasera**, **buonanotte**, (*good morning*, *good evening*, *good night*).
- ▶ Experiment with words. Use the words that you learn in new contexts and find out if they are correct.

4 Grammar

- ▶ To organize the study of grammar write your own grammar glossary and add new information and examples as you go along.
- ▶ Experiment with grammar rules. Sit back and reflect on the rules you learn. See how they compare with your own language or other languages you may already speak. Try to find out some rules on your own and be ready to spot the exceptions. By doing this you'll remember the rules better and get a feel for the language. Try to find examples of grammar in conversations or other articles.
- ▶ Keep a 'pattern bank' that organizes examples which can be listed under the structures you've learned.
- ▶ Use old vocabulary to practise new grammar structures.
- ▶ When you learn a new verb form, write the conjugation of several different verbs you know that follow the same form.

5 Pronunciation

- ▶ When organizing the study of pronunciation keep a section of your notebook for pronunciation rules and practise those that trouble you.
- ▶ Repeat all of the conversations, line by line. Listen to yourself and try to mimic what you hear.
- ▶ Record yourself and compare yourself to a native speaker.
- ▶ Make a list of words that you find difficult and practise them.
- ▶ Study individual sounds, then full words.
- ▶ Don't forget, it's not just about pronouncing letters and words correctly, but using the right intonation. So, when practising words and sentences, mimic the rising and falling intonation of native speakers.

6 Listening and reading

The conversations in this book include questions to help guide you in your understanding. But you can go further by following some of these tips.

▶ **Imagine the situation.** When listening to or reading the conversations, try to imagine where the scene is taking place and who the main characters are. Let your experience of the world help you guess the meaning of the conversation, e.g. if a conversation takes place in a snack bar you can predict the kind of vocabulary that is being used.

▶ **Concentrate on the main part.** When watching a foreign film you usually get the meaning of the whole story from a few individual shots. Understanding a foreign conversation or article is similar. Concentrate on the main parts to get the message and don't worry about individual words.

▶ **Guess the key words; if you cannot, ask or look them up.** When there are key words you don't understand, try to guess what they mean from the context. If you're listening to an Italian speaker and cannot get the gist of a whole passage because of one word or phrase, try to repeat that word with a questioning tone; the speaker will probably paraphrase it, giving you the chance to understand it. If for example you wanted to find out the meaning of the word **viaggiare** (*to travel*) you would ask **Che cosa vuol dire viaggiare?**

7 Speaking

Rehearse in the foreign language. As all language teachers will assure you, the successful learners are those students who overcome their inhibitions and get into situations where they must speak, write and listen to the foreign language. Here are some useful tips to help you practise speaking Italian:

▶ Hold a conversation with yourself, using the conversations of the units as models and the structures you have learnt previously.

▶ After you have conducted a transaction with a salesperson, clerk or waiter in your own language, pretend that you have to do it in Italian e.g. *buying groceries, ordering food, drinks* and so on.

▶ Look at objects around you and try to name them in Italian.

▶ Look at people around you and try to describe them in detail.

▶ Try to answer all of the questions in the book out loud.

- Say the dialogues out loud then try to replace sentences with ones that are true for you.
- Try to role play different situations in the book.

8 Learn from your errors

Don't let errors interfere with getting your message across. Making errors is part of any normal learning process, but some people get so worried that they won't say anything unless they are sure it is correct. This leads to a vicious circle as the less they say, the less practice they get and the more mistakes they make.

Note the seriousness of errors. Many errors are not serious as they do not affect the meaning; for example if you use the wrong article (e.g. **il** for **la**), wrong pronouns (**la finisco domani** for **lo finisco domani**) or wrong adjective ending (**giallo** for **gialla**). So concentrate on getting your message across and learn from your mistakes.

9 Learn to cope with uncertainty

- **Don't over-use your dictionary.**
  When reading a text in the foreign language, don't be tempted to look up every word you don't know. Underline the words you do not understand and read the passage several times, concentrating on trying to get the gist of the passage. If after the third time there are still words which prevent you from getting the general meaning of the passage, look them up in the dictionary.
- **Don't panic if you don't understand.**
  If at some point you feel you don't understand what you are told, don't panic or give up listening. Either try and guess what is being said and keep following the conversation or, if you cannot, isolate the expression or words you haven't understood and have them explained to you. The speaker might paraphrase them and the conversation will carry on.
- **Keep talking.**
  The best way to improve your fluency in the foreign language is to talk every time you have the opportunity to do so: keep the conversations flowing and don't worry about the mistakes. If you get stuck for a particular word, don't let the conversation stop; paraphrase or replace the unknown word with one you do know, even if you have to simplify what you want to say. As a last resort use the word from your own language and pronounce it in the foreign accent.

Useful expressions

GREETINGS, FAREWELLS AND OTHER USEFUL EXPRESSIONS

good morning	**buon giorno/buongiorno**
good afternoon/evening	**buona sera/buonasera**
good night	**buona notte/buonanotte**
goodbye	**arrivederci**
hello/goodbye	**ciao** *(informal)*
see you later	**ci vediamo più tardi**
yes	**sì**
no	**no**
please	**per favore**
thank you	**grazie**
you're welcome	**prego**
pardon?	**prego?**
excuse me	**scusi**
OK	**va bene**
My name is…	**Mi chiamo…**
How old is he/she/it?	**Quanti anni ha?**
He/she/it is X years old.	**Ha X anni.**
Pleased to meet you.	**Piacere**.
today	**oggi**
tomorrow	**domani**
yesterday	**ieri**
for a week	**per una settimana**

SURVIVAL PHRASES

Can you repeat, please?	**Può ripetere, per favore?**
Can you speak more slowly?	**Può parlare più lentamente?**
I'm sorry (but) I don't understand.	**Mi dispiace, ma non capisco.**
I'm sorry (but) I don't speak Italian very well.	**Mi dispiace, ma non parlo molto bene l'italiano.**
Do you speak English?	**Parla inglese?**
What does X mean?	**Che cosa significa/vuol dire X?**
Can you help me?	**Mi può aiutare?**
I'm a foreigner.	**Sono straniero/a.**
I don't know.	**Non lo so.**

SERVICES AND TRAVEL

How much does it/do they cost?	**Quanto costa/costano?**
Where is the ticket office?	**Dov'è la biglietteria?**
Where does the coach/bus for the city centre leave from?	**Da dove parte il pullman/l'autobus per il centro?**
Which platform does it leave from?	**Da quale binario parte?**
It leaves from…	**Parte da…**
Where's the taxi stand?	**Dov'è il posteggio dei tassì?**
When does the train to X leave?	**A che ora parte il treno per X?**
Can you tell me the way to X?	**Mi può indicare la strada per X?**
You have to change at X.	**Deve cambiare a X.**
Does the train stop at X?	**Il treno si ferma a X?**
What time does the chemist's/bank shut?	**A che ora chiude la farmacia/la banca?**
I would like…	**Vorrei…**
You must pay at the cash desk.	**Deve pagare alla cassa.**
You must get the receipt first.	**Deve prima fare lo scontrino.**
Where is the nearest supermarket?	**Dov' è il supermercato più vicino?**
How long does it take on foot?	**Quanto tempo ci vuole a piedi?**
Where can I buy…?	**Dove posso comprare…?**
Does the hotel have free parking?	**L'albergo ha un parcheggio gratuito?**
It costs X euros a day.	**Costa X euro al giorno.**
Please give me the number-plate of your car.	**Mi può dare la targa della Sua auto/macchina?**
I/we have a reservation.	**Ho/abbiamo una prenotazione.**
Please sign here.	**Una firma qui, per favore.**
I don't like…	**Non mi piace…**
I'm allergic to…	**Sono allergico/a a…**
I don't/He/she doesn't feel very well.	**Non mi sento/si sente molto bene.**
I feel sick.	**Ho la nausea.**
Do you have a table for X?	**Ha un tavolo per X?**
We are in a bit of a hurry.	**Abbiamo un po' di fretta.**
Can I pay by credit card?	**Posso pagare con la carta di credito?**
There's a X kilometre queue.	**C'è una coda di x kilometri.**
There's been an accident.	**C'è stata un'incidente.**
Where's the hospital/casualty?	**Dov'e' l'ospedale/il Pronto Soccorso?**
I need…	**Mi serve…**
I need a charger for my mobile phone.	**Mi serve un caricabatteria per il mio cellulare.**
I need to recharge my mobile phone.	**Devo ricaricare il mio cellulare.**

Pronunciation guide

00.01

Italian is always pronounced as it is spelled. Once you have learned the following rules relating to how the letters and vowels sound, you will find the pronunciation of every new word quite straightforward.

It should be noted that, with very few exceptions, all true Italian words end in a vowel and that all vowels must be pronounced – including an **e** when it occurs at the end of a word. The Italian alphabet uses only 21 letters: **k**, **w**, **x** and **y** are used only in foreign words. **J** is nowadays confined to a few place names (e.g. **Jesolo**) and surnames (e.g. **Tajoli**).

Listen to the recording and repeat out loud each sound and the Italian words given in the examples.

The English sounds given below as a guide are those used in standard southern English.

VOWELS

a	as **a** in b**a**th	c**a**sa **a**rtist**a**
e	*has two sounds:*	
	as **e** *in* w**e**ll	b**e**llo, v**e**nto
	as **e** *in* th**e**y	v**e**rde, p**e**nna
i	*as* **i** *in* mach**i**ne	l**i**ra p**i**zza
o	*has two sounds:*	
	as **o** *in* n**o**t	p**o**sta, **o**pera
	as **o** *in* f**o**rt	t**o**tale, s**o**mma
u	*as* **u** *in* r**u**le	t**u**rista l**u**na

> **TIP**
> Although these are the rules, you will find that the pronunciation of **e** and **o** can vary from region to region. This is because dialects influence pronunciation.

CONSONANTS

c	*has two sounds:*	
	before e or i, as **ch** *in* **ch**illy	c̲ena, c̲iao
	before **h**, **a**, **o** or **u**, *as* **ch** *in* **ch**emist	c̲hiave, c̲osa, sc̲usi
g	*has two sounds:*	
	before e or i, as **g** *in* **g**entile	g̲entile, g̲iardino
	before **h**, **a**, **o** or **u**, *as* **g** *in* **g**arden	g̲ondola, spag̲hetti
h	*is never pronounced. When it follows* **c** *or* **g**, it gives them a hard sound (see letters **c** and **g** above).	
r	*is always rolled as in Scottish English*	car̲ne, r̲aro
s	*has two sounds:*	
	as **s** *in* **s**et	s̲icuro, s̲ì
	as **se** *in* ro**se**	ros̲a, mus̲ica
z	*has two sounds:*	
	as **ts** *in* pe**ts**	graz̲ie, staz̲ione
	as **tz** *in* **tz**ar	z̲ero, z̲ona

DOUBLE CONSONANTS

These are pronounced as the single consonant, but with a slightly longer sound. See if you can produce/hear the difference:

pal̲a, pal̲la; don̲a, don̲na; som̲a, som̲ma; pap̲a, pap̲pa; car̲o, car̲ro.

TIP
Another way to remember how to pronounce **c** and **g** is that they have a *soft* sound before **e** and **i**; in all other cases, they have a *hard* sound.

00.04
COMBINED LETTERS

ch	as <u>ch</u> in ar<u>ch</u>itect	<u>ch</u>iave
gh	as **g** in **g**et	spa<u>gh</u>etti
gli	as **lli** in bri**lli**ant	gi<u>gli</u>
gn	as **ni** in o**ni**on	ba<u>gn</u>o, si<u>gn</u>ora
qu	as <u>qu</u> in <u>qu</u>ality	<u>qu</u>ando, <u>qu</u>adro
sc	*has two sounds:*	
	when followed by **e** *or* **i**, *as* <u>**sh**</u> *in* <u>**sh**</u>oe	<u>sc</u>ialle, <u>sc</u>ena
	when followed by **h**, **a**, **o** *or* **u**, *as* <u>**sk**</u> *in* <u>**sk**</u>y	<u>sc</u>uola, <u>sc</u>olaro

STRESS

As you know, many words consist of two or more syllables joined together, for example **bi-cy-cle**. When you pronounce a word, you put stress on (i.e. emphasize) a particular syllable of the word. **Bi-cy-cle**, for instance, is stressed on the first syllable and sounds very odd if the stress is wrongly placed.

Getting the stress in the right place is an important aspect of making yourself understood in a foreign language, but it is relatively easy in Italian, as most Italian words are stressed on the syllable before last, as in **bi-ci-<u>clet</u>-ta**. When the stress falls on the last syllable, an accent is placed above it: **cit<u>tà</u>**, **quali<u>tà</u>**.

Sometimes the stress is on the third or even the fourth syllable from the end, and as there is no fixed rule for these words, you will have to memorize them. In this book, the stressed syllables are underlined to help you with such words, e.g. **<u>Na</u>poli**.

SOME ADVICE ON MASTERING PRONUNCIATION

If you have difficulty in pronouncing a word, try to relax as much as possible (particularly the facial muscles) and divide it into syllables: **cameriere** *waiter* will become **ca-me-rie-re**. However, it is not important that you should acquire perfect pronunciation immediately. The aim, as previously mentioned, is to be understood. Here are a number of techniques for learning pronunciation.

1 **Listen carefully to the recording and to native speakers or teachers. If possible, repeat the dialogues out loud, pretending that you are a native speaker of Italian.**

2 **Record your voice and compare your pronunciation with examples spoken by native Italians.**

3 **If possible, ask native speakers to listen to your pronunciation and tell you how to improve it. If in great difficulty with a particular sound, ask a native speaker how it is formed. Watch how they shape it, then practise it in front of a mirror.**

4 **Make a list of words that give you pronunciation problems and practise them.**

5 **Practise the sounds on their own and then use them progressively in words, sentences and tongue-twisters such as tre tigri contro tre tigri** *three tigers versus three tigers.*

PRACTICE

 00.05

Practise saying out loud the names of the places below and look at the map at the end of the book to see where they are:

Aosta	Ancona	Torino	Perugia
Genova	L'Aquila	Milano	Roma
Trento	Napoli	Trieste	Bari
Venezia	Potenza	Bologna	Catanzaro
Firenze	Palermo	Pisa	Capri
Siena	Ischia	Cagliari	San Gimignano

Come sta?

How are you?

In this unit, you will learn how to:
▶ *say hello and goodbye.*
▶ *exchange greetings.*
▶ *say please and thank you.*
▶ *ask people to speak more slowly.*
▶ *make a simple apology.*

CEFR: (A1) *Can make an introduction and use basic greeting and leave-taking expressions.*

I saluti *Greetings*

Italy is a beautiful country blessed not only with some of the most stunning countryside and cities in the world, but also with very friendly and hospitable people, who are more than happy to help out. However, it is important to note that there are certain codes of conduct which Italians like everyone to observe, beginning with levels of formality in their language. Whereas in English respect is conveyed by the construction used, in Italian the level of formality with someone is shown by the form of *you*, which is chosen by the speaker. The general rule is to use **tu** only with close friends, family and children, and the formal **Lei** with anyone else. It is better to err on the side of formality. Similarly, using the informal **ciao** when entering or leaving a shop where you don't know the staff could be considered rude. In terms of physical greetings, Italians tend to shake hands to greet each other. If they are close friends or relatives, they may kiss on both cheeks (also males greeting males). So, **Benvenuto**! – *Welcome!*

What are the two meanings of *ciao*? (Look in the Key for the answer.)

Vocabulary builder

Look at the words and complete the missing expressions. Then listen to all the words.

GREETINGS

buongiorno/buon giorno	*good morning/good day/good afternoon*
buonasera/buona sera	*good evening/good afternoon*
buonanotte/buona notte	*good night*
arrivederci	*goodbye/see you soon*
ciao	*hello/hi/so long/cheerio* (i.e. informal 'hello')
per favore	*please*
grazie	*thank you* (this can be used after **sì** as well as after *no*)
Come sta?/Come stai?	*How are you?* (formal/informal)
bene, grazie	*well/fine, thank you*
e	*and*
E _____?	*And you?* (informal)
E _____?	*And you?* (formal)

> **TIP**
> Look back at section **I saluti**/*Greetings* to find help with the answers!

Now make a simple dialogue by filling in the blanks with the Italian for the expressions in the right-hand column (Check the Key for the answer.).

Remo	_____, Lucia!	Hello, Lucia!
Lucia	_____, Remo!	Good morning, Remo!
Lucia	_____?	How are you?
Remo	_____.	Fine, thanks.

Here are some other words you will find useful in greetings situations.

signore	*sir/gentleman*
signor	*Mr*
signora	*madam/Mrs/Ms*
signorina	*Miss/young woman/young lady*
arrivederla	*goodbye* (formal)
sì	*yes*
no	*no*
scusi	*sorry/excuse me* (also to attract attention)
mi dispiace	*I am sorry/I beg your pardon*
molto bene	*very well/very good*
non	*not*
non troppo bene	*not too well*
non c'è male	*not too bad* (**c'è** is pronounced as **che** in cherry)
inglese	*English*
parlare	*to speak*
Parla inglese?	*Do you speak English?*
più lentamente	*more slowly*

In this exercise, match the English to the Italian. Try not to look back until you've finished. The first one is done for you.

a	good evening		**1**	mi dispiace
b	thank you		**2**	per favore
c	I'm sorry		**3**	buona sera
d	good morning		**4**	scusi
e	excuse me		**5**	grazie
f	please		**6**	buongiorno

Dialoghi *Dialogues*

01.03 **Is it morning or evening? Listen to the following dialogues before practising them as suggested.**

Signora Verdi	Buongiorno, signor Brunetti.
Signor Brunetti	Buongiorno, signora Verdi. Come sta?
Signora Verdi	Bene, grazie. E Lei?
Signor Brunetti	Molto bene. Arrivederla, signora.
Signora Verdi	Arrivederla.

 Play the parts of both signora Verdi and signor Brunetti and repeat the dialogue until you are confident about it, remembering the intonation for making questions.

DIALOGO 2

01.04 **Does signorina Bini speak English?**

Mr Jones	Scusi, parla inglese?
Signorina Bini	Sì, molto bene.
Mr Jones	Parli più lentamente, per favore!

 Now play the parts of both Mr Jones and signorina Bini, paying particular attention to pronouncing the question. Can you repeat this dialogue without looking at it?

DIALOGO 3

01.05 **How is signora Massa?**

You	Buonasera, signora, come sta?
Signora Massa	Non troppo bene.
You	Mi dispiace!
Signora Massa	E Lei, come sta?
You	Non c'è male, grazie.

Language discovery

Look back at the dialogues. Can you find an expression that means *And you?* **Are the conversations formal or informal? (Check in the Key for the answer.)**

1 GREETINGS AND LEAVE-TAKING

Buongiorno (or **buon giorno**) is used until about 4 p.m. in summer or when it's getting dark in winter, after which **buonasera** (or **buona sera**) is used. In central and southern Italy, **buonasera** is normally used from 1 p.m. Both greetings are used when meeting or leaving someone. **Buonanotte** (or **buona notte**) is only used when taking one's leave at night or before going to bed. **Buon pomeriggio** (*good afternoon*) is only used in very formal situations such as on the TV news.

Arrivederci is used when taking leave from a person you wish to or may see again; you could also use it when leaving a shop. **Arrivederla** is much more formal and is used to show greater regard for the person. **Ciao** means both *hello* and *goodbye*, and is used only among close friends, members of one's family and with children, as it is very informal.

Younger people (up to approximately mid-twenties) often use the informal **tu**, even when addressing strangers of about the same age or younger. When young people meet, as well as the informal **ciao**, **salve** is often used. **Salve** is a useful word which is a sort of halfway house between **ciao** and **buongiorno**. It conveys respect but is used in situations which are less formal or when meeting people of your own age. It can be used both when arriving and leaving. When leaving in a informal context, you can also use **ciao**, **ci vediamo** (*see you*), or **a presto** (*see you soon*).

2 MR AND MRS

Remember that **signor** means *Mr*, so it's always followed by a man's name. (When addressing a man without using his name, use **signore**.) When calling or talking to a person in a formal way, say: **signor Verdi**, **signora Verdi**, **signorina Verdi**. When referring to yourself (in a formal way) or others, say **il signor**…, **la signora**…, **la signorina**…: **Io sono la signora Nelson**. In Italian, it is quite polite to call a young woman who is not married **signorina**, but the tendency is to call an adult woman **signora** whether she is married or not.

3 ASKING QUESTIONS

To ask a question in Italian, you simply raise the pitch of your voice at the end of the sentence. When writing, you just add a question mark at the end.

On the audio there was a word which changed its meaning when the intonation changed – what was it? Look in the Key for the answer.

PRATICA *PRACTICE*

1 How would you say hello to the following people at the times shown? Remember to add **signore**, **signora** or **signorina**.

    a 6 p.m.   **b** 11 a.m.   **c** 10 p.m.

   _____   _____   _____

2 It is late at night and you decide to go to bed. What would you say to your host?

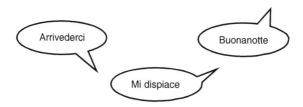

Arrivederci

Buonanotte

Mi dispiace

3 A vendor in the market is trying to sell you a leather jacket, but you are not interested. What do you say?

Prego

No, grazie

Mi dispiace

Arrivederci

4 **A woman inadvertently drops a banknote on the pavement; you wish to attract her attention.**

  a What do you say? _____

  b She turns, and you point at the note on the pavement. She thanks you. What do you answer?_____

  c Now she asks you a question: you don't hear it properly. What do you say? _____

  d You are still uncertain of what she is saying: she is speaking too fast. What do you ask her to do?

    _____ **per favore**.

  e She wants to know if you speak English: what does she say?

    _____ ?

5 **Use the clues to complete the grid and find, in the vertical shaded box, a word which is used when you want someone to repeat something which you have not quite heard or understood.**

  a You've spilt some wine. You begin your apology by saying...

  b You greet someone after 4 p.m.

  c The answer to **grazie**.

  d You are asked **Come sta**?

  e What you add when asking a favour.

  f *And you?*

? Test yourself

01.06 Before listening to the recording, try to fill in the answers. What would you say if:

1 you wish to attract someone's attention?

2 you meet an Italian acquaintance in the late afternoon?

3 someone thanks you?

4 you want something repeated?

5 you step on someone's foot?

6 an acquaintance asks how you are and you wish to know how he/she is?

7 you wish to know whether a shop assistant speaks English?

8 someone is speaking too fast?

9 you say good night to Mr Bini?

10 you wish to refuse/accept something offered to you?

Check the answers in the **Key to the exercises and tests** at the end of the book. If you've got them all right, you are ready to move on to Unit 2. If you found the test difficult, spend more time revising Unit 1. Follow this principle throughout Units 1–10, and you'll know that you are building up a reliable bank of knowledge.

SELF CHECK

I CAN. . .
. . . greet someone
. . . thank and be thanked
. . . ask someone if they speak English
. . . apologize simply
. . . ask someone to speak more slowly
. . . politely attract someone's attention

1 Come sta? *How are you?*   **9**

Come si chiama?
What's your name?

In this unit, you will learn how to:
▶ *say who you are.*
▶ *ask who other people are.*
▶ *deny something.*
▶ *enquire about someone's nationality and tell them your own.*

CEFR: (A1) *Can introduce yourself and others, and can ask and answer questions about personal details.*

Review

Before you carry on with Unit 2, check to see if you remember how to:
1 ask someone how he/she is?
2 say 'I beg your pardon'?
3 ask someone to repeat something?

Check in the Key for the answers.

Titles *I titoli*

In Italy, titles are given far greater importance than in English-speaking countries, and are used much more frequently. Consequently, in business circles titles and surnames are still used. All university graduates – not just graduates in the medical profession or PhDs – are entitled to be called **dottore** (*men*) or **dottoressa** (*women*). Secondary and tertiary teachers (who must be graduates) are called **professore** (*men*) or **professoressa** (*women*). Architects, engineering graduates and lawyers are called **architetto**, **ingegnere** and **avvocato** (*men*) or **avvocatessa** (*women*). For this reason, it is quite common to hear: **Buongiorno, dottoressa!** or **Come sta, architetto?** In southern Italy, the title of **dottore** is sometimes used when talking to a man whom one doesn't know but to whom one wishes to show great respect, even if he is not **dottore**.

 Now have a look at the brief exchange in the drawing above. What do you notice about the titles? Look in the Key for the answer!

Vocabulary builder

 02.01 **Look at the words and phrases below and see if you can complete the missing English expressions. Then listen to them and repeat them out loud.**

INTRODUCTIONS

come	*how/what*
mi chiamo	*my name is*
si chiama	*he/she/it is called; you are called* (formal)
ti chiami	*you _____*
Come si chiama?	*What's his/her/your name?* (formal)
è	*he/she/it is; you are* (formal)
(io) sono	*I am*
non	*_____*
non sono	*I am _____*
non è	*he/she/it is not; you are not* (formal)

NEW EXPRESSIONS

chi?	*who?*
Chi è Lei?	*Who are you?* (formal – note the capital 'L')
Chi è lei?	*Who is she?*
Chi è lui?	*Who is he?*
che	*who/whom/which/that*
questo è/questa è	*this is*
bambino/bambina	*child (boy)/child (girl)*
Piacere	*Pleased to meet you.*
si accomodi/s'accomodi	*come in, please; do sit down*
soltanto	*only*
ma	*but*
mia moglie	*my wife*
mio marito	*my husband*
nostra figlia	*our daughter*
nostro figlio	*our son*
straniero/a	*foreign man/woman*
padre	*father*
madre	*mother*
fratello	*brother*
sorella	*sister*

TIP
Sometimes a letter will be underlined – for example the first 'o' in **Si accomodi**: this indicates where the stress is to be placed in a word that does not follow the rules in the Pronunciation guide.

 **Dialoghi** *Dialogues*

Sergio and Francesca are having a party at their home in Genova. The guests mingle and chat to each other. Listen and follow the text.

1 02.02 **Do the people at the party use formal or informal language?**

Paolo Marchi	Come si chiama?
Jackie Jones	Mi chiamo Jackie Jones.
	E Lei, come si chiama?
Paolo Marchi	Io sono Paolo Marchi.

DIALOGO 2

2 02.03 **In this conversation, Mr Dean has mistaken signora Chiarella for another lady. Who has he mistaken her for?**

Mr Dean	Scusi, Lei è la signora Pucci?
Angela Chiarella	No, non sono la signora Pucci.
Mr Dean	Come si chiama?
Angela Chiarella	Mi chiamo Angela Chiarella.

> **TIP**
> *No, I am not*: remember to say **No, non sono…** and not just **Non sono…** or **No sono…**

3 **Now, find the expressions in the conversation that mean:**
   a What's your name? _____
   b My name is… _____
   c No, I am not… _____
   d And you, what's your name? _____

 4 **Now cover up your answers and see if you can say them without looking at the conversation.**

The party is still going on at Sergio and Francesca's home. Listen and follow the text.

DIALOGO 3

5 02.04 **Does signora Chiarella speak a foreign language?**

Angela Chiarella	Chi è la signorina che parla inglese?
Mr Dean	È Susan White. Lei parla inglese?
Angela Chiarella	No, mi dispiace ma non parlo inglese; parlo soltanto italiano.

DIALOGO 4

6 02.05 **Sergio approaches Mr Dean and introduces his wife and a young girl to him. What's the young girl's name and how is she related to the couple?**

Sergio	Questa è mia moglie Francesca.
Mr Dean	Piacere.
Francesca	Piacere.
Mr Dean	E la bambina, chi è?
Sergio	Questa è nostra figlia; si chiama Valentina.

7 **Decide whether each of these statements is true or false.**
   a Angela can speak English.
   b Sergio's daughter is called Francesca.
   c The lady who speaks English is called Susan White.
   d Mr Dean has met Sergio's wife and daughter before.

> **TIP**
> Remember that **chi** is used in questions, and also that **che** (*that/which*) can never be omitted as it sometimes is in English: **la lingua che parlo –** *the language (that) I speak.*

8 **Review the expressions below from the conversations. Then match them to the English meaning.**
   a Questa è nostra figlia.
   b Lei parla inglese?
   c Piacere.
   d No, mi dispiace.
   e Parlo soltanto italiano.

   1 Do you speak English?
   2 I only speak Italian.
   3 No, I'm sorry.
   4 This is our daughter.
   5 Pleased to meet you.

# Language discovery

Look in the dialogues for the three words listed below. What word precedes them? What do you think is the meaning of the word? Is it used with masculine or feminine words?

a _____ signora
b _____ signorina
c _____ bambina

Now can you work out which of these words for a/an/one is *masculine* (m.) and which is *feminine* (f.): una and un. Check below!

1 IL, LA

Il is used before masculine nouns (**il treno** *the train*, **il cane** *the dog*, **il libro** *the book*) and **la** before feminine nouns (**la posta** *the mail*, **la mamma** *the mum*, **la voce** *the voice*). **L'** is used instead of **la** before a noun starting with a vowel.

2 UN, UNA

Un is used before masculine nouns (**un treno** *a train*, **un signore** *a gentleman*) and **una** before feminine ones (**una lettera** *a letter*, **una penna** *a pen*).

 Now look back at Units 1 and 2 so far, and write down two other words that you think are masculine and two that are feminine. (You can check in the Vocabulary at the end of the book.)

3 NOUNS

Most names for things in the singular end in either **-o** or **-a** (**museo** *museum*, **mamma** *mum*). When they end in **-o**, they are mostly masculine nouns (**vino** *wine*); when they end in **-a**, they are mostly feminine nouns (**banca** *bank*). This distinction is called 'gender'.

Some nouns end in **-e**: these can be either masculine or feminine, and you will learn these as you meet them e.g. **tenore** (m.) *tenor*, **voce** (f.) *voice*. In Italian, names for men usually end in **-o** (**Sergio**), while names for women usually end in **-a** (**Angela**).

4 ADJECTIVES

Words which qualify (describe) a noun are called adjectives. In **Questa penna è rossa** *This pen is red*, **rossa** is the adjective which describes **penna**.

In Italian, adjectives, like nouns, can be either masculine or feminine; since **penna** is feminine, **rossa** needs to be feminine too. In **Questo vestito è rosso** *This dress is red*, since the noun **vestito** is masculine, the adjective **rosso** also needs to be masculine. This is called the agreement of the adjectives with the nouns.

The same rule applies to words describing one's nationality. Adjectives of nationality do not require a capital letter.

Sergio says: nostra figlia *our daughter.* **Try translating into Italian, using the correct form of ricco** *rich: Our daughter is rich*. **Check your answer in the Key.**

NAZIONALITÀ *NATIONALITIES*

02.06 While you are reading and listening to the recording, try to work out the special rule relating to nationalities ending in –ese.

TIP
When you want to say *me too*, use **anch'io.**

Lei è . . .	Lui è . . .	
australiana	australiano	*Australian*
austriaca	austriaco	*Austrian*
tedesca	tedesco	*German*
spagnola	spagnolo	*Spanish*
svizzera	svizzero	*Swiss*
britannica	britannico	*British*
inglese	inglese	*English*
americana	americano	*American*
scozzese	scozzese	*Scottish*
gallese	gallese	*Welsh*
irlandese	irlandese	*Irish*
portoghese	portoghese	*Portuguese*
neozelandese	neozelandese	*a New Zealander*
canadese	canadese	*Canadian*
francese	francese	*French*

Did you get it? Adjectives of nationality ending in **-ese** have the same form whether they are masculine or feminine.

5 QUESTO, QUESTA

Using dialogue 4 to help you, see if you can translate this sentence into Italian: *This is our son.* _____

Questo and **questa** are used before masculine and feminine nouns respectively:

Questo		il duomo.		*the cathedral.*
	è	un ombrello.	*This is*	*an umbrella.*
Questa		la banca.		*the bank.*
		una chiesa.		*a church.*

Words that express *action* or *being*, such as **parlo**, **sono** and **è**, are called verbs. To deny something, just put **non** before the verb: **Sono tedesco** *I am German*, **Non sono tedesco** *I am not German*.

In English, verbs are often preceded by words such as *I, you, he, she,* etc.; these are called subject pronouns. They are not used in Italian (except for the formal **Lei**) unless special emphasis is required: **Io sono il signor Verdi**, *Lei* **chi è?** (or, because in Italian the word order can be more flexible, you could say **Chi è Lei?**).

If you consult the dictionary to look up the verb *to speak*, you find **parlare**. This form of the verb does not indicate who is doing the action; it is called the infinitive of the verb. In Italian, infinitives fall into three groups: verbs ending in **-are** (e.g. **studiare** *to study*), which are the most numerous, verbs ending in **-ere** (e.g. **vendere** *to sell*) and verbs ending in **-ire** (e.g. **partire** *to leave*).

> **TIP**
> There is usually no difference in Italian between *I speak* and *I am speaking*: for both you can say **parlo**.

When speaking about yourself in the present (present tense), you change the ending (**-are, -ere, -ire**) into an **-o**: **parlo** *I speak*; **vendo** *I sell*; **parto** *I leave*. This part of the verb is called the first person singular

To form the present tense for *you* (formal), *he, she* or *it*, you replace the ending with **-a** (verbs whose infinitive ends in **-are**) or **-e** (verbs with infinitives ending in -**ere** and -**ire**): **parla** *you speak, he/she speaks*; **vende** *you sell, he/she sells*; **parte** *you leave, he/she leaves*. This is the third person singular.

To form the present tense for *we*, replace the ending with **-iamo**: **parliamo** *we speak*; **vendiamo** *we sell*; **partiamo** *we leave*. This is called the first person plural.

Here's a summary of the forms you have met so far of a regular verb of the first type:

parlare *to speak*	
(io) parlo	*I speak*
(tu) parli	*you* (informal) *speak*
(lui, lei) parla	*he/she speaks*
(Lei) parla	*you* (formal) *speak*
(noi) parliamo	*we speak*

PRATICA *PRACTICE*

1 Change the following sentences into negative ones by placing non before the verb.

a James parla italiano.

b Sono Francesca.

c Parlo inglese.

d Valerio è tedesco.

e Il signor Lupi è straniero.

2 Fill in il or la before these nouns. You will probably be able to deduce the meaning of most of these words.

a _____ musica

b _____ parco

c _____ stazione (f.)

d _____ periodo

e _____ cellulare (m.)

f _____ telefono

g _____ pizza

h _____ mercato

i _____ conversazione (f.)

j _____ pasta

TIP
Did you notice that that both **stazione** and **conversazione** were feminine? All nouns ending in –**zione** are feminine in gender!

3 Add either the missing letter -o or -a at the end of the word, or il or la before it. If you want to check the meanings, look in the Vocabulary.

a _____ gioco

b la malatti _____

c il temp _____

d _____ birra

e _____ divertimento

f la trattori _____

4 Fill in **un** or **una** before these nouns.

a _____ persona
b _____ concerto
c _____ edificio
d _____ strada
e _____ porto
f _____ colore (m.)
g _____ gabinetto
h _____ regione (f.)
i _____ teatro

5 Write the appropriate forms of **questo** and **questa** in the spaces. After completing and correcting the exercises, read them out loud until you are satisfied that you have learned them.

a _____ è Angelo.
b _____ è Maria.
c _____ è la banca.
d _____ è il signor Massa.
e _____ è la signorina Jones.
f _____ è mia figlia.

6 What are the nationalities of these men and women?

		abita in	Australia.	è	
	Charline		Australia.	è	australiana
a	Franz		Germania		
b	Alain		Canada		
c	Vasco		Portogallo		
d	John		Inghilterra		
e	Anne		Svizzera		
f	Neil		Galles		
g	Wilma		Austria		
h	Peter		Irlanda		
i	Douglas		Scozia		
j	Nancy		America		
k	Paco		Spagna		
l	Sophie		Francia		

READING

Jenny Fraser has written a note to her new Italian colleague Leonardo, who wants to know about her family.

1 **Can you work out what these words mean? You can check the answers in the Key.**

   a caro
   b marito
   c gatto
   d abbiamo
   e viviamo
   f presto

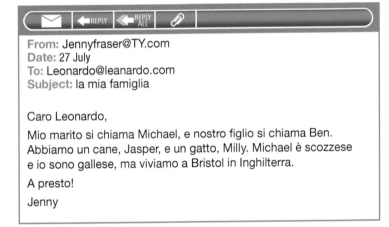

From: Jennyfraser@TY.com
Date: 27 July
To: Leonardo@leanardo.com
Subject: la mia famiglia

Caro Leonardo,

Mio marito si chiama Michael, e nostro figlio si chiama Ben. Abbiamo un cane, Jasper, e un gatto, Milly. Michael è scozzese e io sono gallese, ma viviamo a Bristol in Inghilterra.

A presto!

Jenny

2 **Now answer the questions.**

   a Who is Ben?
   b Where is Jenny from?
   c Who or what is Jasper?
   d Does Jenny expect to see Leonardo soon?

? Test yourself

1 How would you do the following?

  a Ask a person who they are (two ways).
  b Check with a person: 'Is your name …?' (two ways).
  c Ask if a person speaks English (two ways).

2 You have arranged a meeting for 11 a.m. at your Italian hotel with signor Gucci who is your firm's Italian representative. As the clock chimes 11 o'clock, someone is knocking at the door. Fill in the blanks and read your part out loud.

You	*Ask who it is.* _____?
Sig. Gucci	Sono il signor Gucci.
You	*Let him in and greet him.* _____ signor _____, _____ sta?
Sig. Gucci	Bene grazie, e Lei?
You	*Say you are not too bad and tell him to make himself at home.* _____ _____ _____, grazie. Si _____. (You already know how to say 'my wife' **mia moglie**; 'my husband' is **mio marito**.) _____ _____ _____ _____ .
Sig. Gucci	_____ .

SELF CHECK

I CAN. . .
○ . . . say who I am
○ . . . ask someone their name
○ . . . introduce someone
○ . . . deny something
○ . . . tell someone my nationality
○ . . . enquire about someone's nationality

3 Dove abita?

Where do you live?

In this unit, you will learn how to:
▶ *ask where something is.*
▶ *respond if, when asked, you do not know a direction.*
▶ *ask and say where you are from, and where you live.*
▶ *ask other people about their jobs and family.*
▶ *say numbers from 0 to 20.*

CEFR: (A1) *Can ask and answer questions about where he/she lives, people, and can understand sentences and frequently used expressions.*

Review

Francesca visits you while you are in Italy. Complete with some of the things that are said.

1 You ask who is at the door: _____?
2 Francesca thanks you: _____.
3 You ask if Sergio speaks English: _____?

The regions of Italy *Le regioni italiani*

Italy covers an area of 301,336 km² and has about 61 million inhabitants. It is divided into 20 regions, which have a certain degree of autonomy from central government. Five of these regions have a special statute which gives them greater autonomy; these are **Sicilia**, **Sardegna**, **Friuli Venezia-Giulia**, **Trentino Alto-Adige** and **Valle d'Aosta**. The last two regions are bilingual: Italian–German for **Trentino Alto-Adige** and Italian–French for **Valle d'Aosta**. Before the unification of Italy (1861), each region was either an independent state or part of some other European state; for this reason, each region had – and still has – dialects which can differ greatly from each other and from standard Italian. These dialects are reflected in the pronunciation of the official language. Traditions, customs and cuisine also differ greatly from region to region. The advent of television in the early 1950s, and internal migration, prompted a process of standardization which is still going on today. The fact that all the important Italian towns were at some stage in their history the capital of their region explains their enormous artistic wealth.

If the passage you have just read was in Italian, part of one of the sentences would read: **E' divisa in venti regioni…** Can you find this sentence? What do you think **venti** means?

Vocabulary builder

DIRECTIONS AND PLACES

 03.01 **The words below are very useful when you want to talk about where you live or to ask for directions. Read them all and fill in the gaps. Then listen and repeat.**

d_o_ve	*where?*
dov'_è_…?	*where is…?*
via	street
Di dov'_è_?	*Where are you from?* (formal *you*); *Where is he/she from?*
_a_bito	*I live*
_a_bita	*you live* (formal); *he/she/it lives*
_____ _a_bita?	*Where do you live?* (formal); *Where does he/she live?*
non lo so	*I do not know*
non capisco	_____ *understand*
in centro	*in the centre* (of the town)
vicino a	*near, in the proximity of*
piazza	_____

PROFESSIONS

 03.02 You will be meeting these expressions in the dialogues, so first, fill in the gaps whether the word is masculine (m.) or feminine (f.), then try reading the whole list out loud.

lavoro	*I work; work* _____
lavora	*you work; he/she works*
Che lavoro fa?	*What is your job?*
Sono dentista.	*I am a dentist.*
Può consegnare il vino?	*Can you deliver the wine?*
certamente	*certainly*
commessa	*shop assistant/sales clerk* _____

negozio	shop _____
portiere d'albergo	hotel receptionist
insegnante	teacher
insegno	I teach
studente	student
studio	I study; study _____

 ### 03.03 FAMILY MATTERS AND NUMBERS

ho	I have
ha	you have (formal); he/she/it has
Può rispondere a qualche domanda?	Can you answer some questions?
mi dica	go ahead (lit. tell me)
sposato/sposata	married
figlio/figlia	son/daughter
figli/figlie	sons, children/ daughters
quanto/quanta?	how much?
quanti/quante?	how many?
Quanti anni ha?	How old is he/she/it/are you?
Ha 20 anni.	He/she/it is 20 years old.

> **TIP**
> Notice how in Italian, to say how old you are, you use **ho** *I have* rather than **sono** *I am*.

NUMERI DALLO 0 AL 20 *NUMBERS FROM 0 TO 20*

 03.04 **Read and listen. Remember to pay attention to the special stress indicators, for example: dodici.**

0	zero	6	sei	11	undici	16	sedici
1	uno	7	sette	12	dodici	17	diciassette
2	due	8	otto	13	tredici	18	diciotto
3	tre	9	nove	14	quattordici	19	diciannove
4	quattro	10	dieci	15	quindici	20	venti
5	cinque						

> **TIP**
> *Zero, nought* and *0* in telephone numbers are all translated as **zero**. **Un libro** can mean *a book* or *one book*.

Dialoghi *Dialogues*

DIALOGO 1

03.05 **Where is via Mazzini?**

You	Scusi, dov'è via Mazzini?
Primo turista	Mi dispiace ma non lo so: non sono di Genova.
You	Scusi, dov'è via Mazzini?
Secondo turista	Non capisco! Sono straniero!

DIALOGO 2

03.06 **Daniela is carrying out a survey and asks Francesca a few questions. Does Francesca live in Genova or Santa Margherita?**

Daniela	Scusi signora, può rispondere a qualche domanda?
Francesca	Mi dica.
Daniela	Come si chiama?
Francesca	Francesca Ferrari.
Daniela	Di dov'è?
Francesca	Sono di Santa Margherita.
Daniela	Dove abita?
Francesca	Abito a Genova.
Daniela	Lei lavora?
Francesca	Sì, lavoro.
Daniela	Che lavoro fa?
Francesca	Sono dentista.

Decide which of these statements about Francesca in Dialogue 2 are true or false:

a She doesn't have a job.

b Francesca is a doctor.

c She lives in Genova.

DIALOGO 3

03.07 **Is Francesca married? Has she got any children? After listening, check in the Key if you're not sure.**

Daniela	È sposata?
Francesca	Sì.
Daniela	Ha figli?
Francesca	Sì, una bambina.
Daniela	Quanti anni ha la bambina?
Francesca	Ha sei anni.
Daniela	Grazie, signora. Lei è molto gentile.
Francesca	Prego.

DIALOGO 4

03.08 **Sergio, Francesca's husband, has gone to the country to order some wine which is to be delivered. What's his address?**

Sergio	Può consegnare il vino?
Vinaio	Certamente, signore! Dove abita?
Sergio	Abito a Genova, in via Roma.
Vinaio	Numero?
Sergio	Numero 15.
Vinaio	Allora: via Roma, 15 – Genova. Dov'è via Roma?
Sergio	È in centro, vicino a piazza Garibaldi.

DIALOGO 5

03.09 **Daniela asks a group of Italians about their jobs. Does Brunella teach or study mathematics? Look in the Key for the answer.**

Teresa	Sono commessa: lavoro in un negozio.
Piero	Sono portiere d'albergo: lavoro in un albergo.
Brunella	Sono insegnante: insegno matematica.
Claudio	Sono studente: studio medicina.

Language discovery

In Dialogue 3, Francesca talks about her daughter being six years old. How does the ending on the word for *year* anno change to show that it is more than one? Look in the Key for the answer.

1 PLURAL OF NOUNS

When talking of more than one thing, that is to say, in the *plural*, in English, an -*s* is usually added at the end of the noun; in Italian, the plural is made by changing the final vowel of the noun in the following ways:

▶ Nouns ending in **-o** or **-e** normally change to an **-i**:

▷ **libro**, **libri** *book, books*; **automobile** *(f.)*, **automobili** *car, cars*; **cane** *(m.)*, **cani** *dog, dogs*.

▶ Nouns ending in **-a** normally change to an **-e**:

▷ **donna**, **donne** *woman, women*; **ragazza**, **ragazze** *girl, girls*; **domanda**, **domande** *question, questions*.

Ha figli? *Have you got any children?* The plural of **figlio** *son* is **figli**: this is to avoid a double **i** occurring at the end of the word (**zio** *uncle* is one of a few exceptions: its plural is **zii**).

Before plural nouns, **il** and **la** change respectively into **i** and **le**: **il treno**, **i treni** *the train, the trains*; **la casa**, **le case** *the house/home, the houses/homes*. **Questo** and **questa** *this* become **questi** and **queste** *these*; **questo numero**, **questi numeri** *this number, these numbers*.

> **TIP**
> Nouns ending with an accented vowel do not change in the plural:
> **una città** *one town*
> **due città** *two towns*.

2 EITHER GENDER: NOUNS ENDING IN *-ISTA*

Nouns ending in **-ista** can be either masculine or feminine: **il turista/ la turista**; **il violinista/la violinista**. The definite article **il/la** indicates a male or female person.

3 SHOWING GENDER: *SPOSATA/SPOSATO*

To a woman	È sposata?	*Are you married?*
She replies	Sì, sono sposata or No, non sono sposata.	*Yes, I'm married or No, I'm not married.*
To a man	È sposato?	
He replies	Sì, sono sposato or No, non sono sposato.	

> **TIP**
> Verbs ending in **-iare** (e.g. **mangiare** *to eat*, **studiare** *to study*, etc.) take only one **-i** in the **tu** and **noi** forms: **mangi**, **mangiamo**.

4 DROPPING VOWELS: *DOV'È?*

When the last letter of one word and the first letter of the next word are vowels, at times the first vowel is dropped and replaced by an apostrophe ('), e.g. **la arancia** *the orange* becomes **l'arancia**.

In **dove**, the stress falls on the **-o**, whereas **dov'è**? is stressed on the final **-è**. Read these phrases out loud a few times stressing the underlined vowel:

Dove abita? Dov'è il professore?

5   DOVE ABITA? *WHERE DO YOU LIVE?*

Dove abita? The answer is **abito *a*** followed by the name of the city, town, village or small island; **abito *in*** followed by the name of the continent, country, region, county or large island.

Abito *a* Roma.	Abito *in* Europa.
Abito *a* Siena.	Abito *in* Italia.
Abito *a* Portofino.	Abito *in* Toscana.
Abito *a* Capri.	Abito *in* Surrey.
Abito *a* Londra.	Abito *in* Sicilia.

6   VERBS

Here is the complete pattern for regular verbs of the first type:

parlare to speak	
(io) parlo	*I speak*
(tu) parli	*you* (informal) *speak*
(lui, lei, Lei) parla	*he/she speaks, you* (formal) *speak*
(noi) parliamo	*we speak*
(voi) parlate	*you* (plural informal) *speak*
(loro, Loro) parlano	*they speak, you* (plural formal) *speak*

7   HOW TO SAY 'YOU'

The reason why the verb form used with the formal *you* is the third person singular (e.g. **Lei parla**) derives from old usage when it meant *Your Excellency* (*What does Your Excellency say?*).

When addressing more than one person, the formal form of *you* is **Loro**. However, today the plural informal **voi** tends to be used much more often.

Loro p<u>a</u>rlano inglese?   Do you (plural) speak English?

To summarize: there are four ways of saying *you* in Italian!

tu (singular informal)   **voi** (plural informal)

Lei (singular formal)   **Loro** (plural formal)

8 PROFESSIONI E OCCUPAZIONI *PROFESSIONS AND OCCUPATIONS*

In Dialogue 2, Francesca says Sono dentista to say she's a dentist. She does not say Sono UNA dentista. How would you tell Daniela that you are a *waiter* cameriere? Using what you have learned, how would Aldo say that he is a *dentist*?

In Italian, the '*a*', as in '*I am a + profession*' is omitted. The feminine forms of **dottore** and **studente** are, respectively, **dottoressa** and **studentessa**. M<u>e</u>dico, another word for *doctor*, **negoziante** and **insegnante** apply to both men and women. Other occupations are: **segretario/segretaria** *secretary*; **operaio/operaia** *factory worker*; **impiegato/impiegata** *clerical/office worker*; **cameriere/cameriera** *waiter/waitress*; **casalinga** *housewife*; **infermiere/infermiera** *nurse*; **dirigente** *manager*.

PRATICA *PRACTICE*

1 **Fill in the spaces using il or la. Then read out loud each question and answer that you are sorry, but you don't know. The first one has been done for you.**

   a Scusi, dov'è la banca? Mi dispiace ma non lo so.
   b Scusi, dov'è _____ posta? _____
   c Scusi, dov'è _____ teatro? _____
   d Scusi, dov'è _____ museo?_____
   e Scusi, dov'è _____ parco? _____
   f Scusi, dov'è _____ supermercato?_____

If you did not understand the question, what would you answer?

   g _____ _____.

2 **With the help of the map at the end of the book, fill in the gaps using in and a correctly.**

a Angelo abita _____ Toscana.

b Teresa abita _____ Roma.

c Mario abita _____ Sicilia.

d Sergio abita _____ Genova.

e Francesca abita _____ Liguria.

f Maria abita _____ Capri.

3 **You are at a meeting and are told that one of the participants is Italian. You would like to make his acquaintance.**

a Ask him if he is Italian.

You: _____?

He replies: Sì.

b Ask him where he is from.

You: _____?

He replies: Sono di Pavia.

c Introduce yourself and ask his name.

You: _____?

He replies: Stefano Vinci.

⟨?⟩ Test yourself

What are the questions to these answers? Use formal forms.

1 Sì, sono sposato.

2 Sì, ho figli.

3 Ho tre figli.

4 Sono medico.

5 Sì, sono italiano.

6 Abito a Venezia.

7 Ha otto anni.

8 Sì, lavoro.

9 Sono di Torino.

10 Non lo so, mi spiace.

SELF CHECK

I CAN. . .
○ . . . say where I am from and where I live
○ . . . ask someone where they are from
○ . . . understand and give basic directions
○ . . . ask other people about their job and family
○ . . . say numbers from 0 to 20

R1 Review: Units 1–3

This review unit covers the main vocabulary and expressions, language skills and grammar points in the first three units. You can check your answers at the end of the book.

1 **While sitting in the local café, you start talking to an Italian lady. Say each sentence out loud in Italian, then write it down.**

   a Say your name, your nationality and where you come from.

   b Tell her you are pleased to meet her.

   c Ask her to speak more slowly, please.

   d Ask her if she speaks English.

   e Tell her that you speak English, German and Italian. You are a teacher and you are married.

   f Ask where the bank is.

   g Ask her where Piazza Roma is.

2 **Can you remember which article (il, la, l') goes before these nouns?**

   a posta

   b treno

   c vestito

   d cereale

   e conversazione

   f regione

   g duomo

   h cane

   i chiesa

   j infermiera

3 **Do you know the English equivalent of the following?**

   a Scusi, dov'è il museo?

   b Quanti anni ha il bambino?

   c No, non sono sposato.

   d Non capisco il francese.

   e Sono straniero.

   f Questo signore è molto gentile.

4 Put these nouns into the plural.

a La bambina.

b Il teatro.

c La pizza.

d La stazione.

e La città.

f Il vino.

5 Translate these sentences into Italian.

a We only speak Italian.

b This is my brother (**mio fratello**).

c He's called Pietro.

d Does she live in Switzerland?

e Paola is a shop assistant.

f Caterina has three sons.

6 Correct these sentences.

a Scusi, parli inglese?

b Marie-Claire è francesa.

c Un persona abita in Umbria.

d Sono un dentista.

e Dove il parco?

7 Fill in the missing words, choosing from the words in the box.

Luigi abita _____ centro. _____ vicino; e' _____ di geografia. _____ due _____. Luigi non _____ sposato.

lavora   ha   è   in   insegna   cani

8 Choose the right word to complete each sentence.

a Le (figli/figlie/figlio) di Melania si chiamano Erica, Jessica e Lucia.

b (Questa/questi/queste) sono le regioni d'Italia.

c Mangio soltanto (i cereali/le cereali/la cereale).

Com'è?
How is it?

In this unit, you will learn how to:
▶ *describe something.*
▶ *express ownership.*
▶ *express likes, dislikes and preferences.*
▶ *say numbers from 20 to 1,000.*

CEFR: (A1) *Can give opinions, describe things and talk about possessions.*

Review

Write out the following in complete sentences. Then say them out loud.

    1 Your first name and surname: _____ _____ _____
    2 Your nationality: _____ _____
    3 The town you live in: _____ _____ _____
    4 Your age: _____ _____ _____

Il bar *The bar*

The key feature of most bars in Italy is speed. Unless they are having lunch or there is an outside area, customers usually enjoy their drinks standing at the bar, down it quickly, and then take their leave. Prices are slightly higher if you sit at a table, and in crowded bars such as those in stations and city centres, you often have to pay first before getting your order. You will be instructed to **fare prima lo scontrino**, to *get a receipt first*. Of course, Italy boasts some of the finest coffee in the world, and the famous **espresso** (actually called simply **caffè** by Italians) is just one way of drinking it, **il cappuccino**, of course, being another.

Using what you have studied so far, plus the text on the following page, how would you order an espresso coffee in Italy? Check your answer in the Key.

Vocabulary builder

DESCRIBING THINGS/POSSESSIONS

 04.01 **Look at the list below and fill in the blanks. You will have met these words before. Then listen to the recording and try to learn them.**

Com'è?	*How is (it)?/What's (it) like?*
Che cos'è?	*What is this?*
Qual è la sua automobile?	*Which (one) is your car?*
Di che colore è?	*What _____ is it?*
C'è un telefono qui?	*_____ a telephone here?*
non c'è…	*_____ is no…*
Ci sono negozi qui vicino?	*Are there (any) _____ nearby?*
non ci sono…	*there are no…*
il mio/la _____	*my, mine*
il suo/la sua	*your, yours* (formal); *his; her, hers*
non tutte	*not all of them*

04.02 LIKES, DISLIKES AND PREFERENCES

In Italian, when you want to say that you like something, you use **mi piace** for one thing, and **mi piacciono** for more than one. Look at the first two examples below, then listen to the recording.

Mi piace la pizza	*I like pizza.*
Mi piacciono i lamponi	*I like raspberries.*
mi piace, mi piacciono	*I like (it), I like (them)*
non mi piace/piacciono	*I do not like it/them*
zucchero/tè (m.)	*sugar/tea*
acqua/vino/birra	*water/wine/beer*
pane (m.)/latte (m.)/frutta	*bread/milk/fruit*
treni	*trains*
bibite/limoni	*soft drinks/lemons*
Le piace il caffè?	*Do you* (formal) *like coffee?*
Le piacciono i biscotti?	*Do you* (formal) *like biscuits/cookies?*
Preferisco le paste.	*I prefer cakes/pastries.*
molto/troppo	*very/too much*
andare a teatro	*to go to the theatre*

> **TIP**
> **Mi piace** may also be used with the infinitive of any verb, e.g. **Mi piace parlare italiano** *I like speaking Italian.*

20 **venti**	50 **cinquanta**	80 **ottanta**	200 **duecento**
30 **trenta**	60 **sessanta**	90 **novanta**	300 **trecento**
40 **quaranta**	70 **settanta**	100 **cento**	1,000 **mille**

To form all the other numbers in between, combine hundreds, tens and units:

26 **ventisei**	67 **sessantasette**	356 **trecentocinquantasei**

The final vowel of the tens is omitted before **uno** and **otto**: **ventuno**, **ventotto**; **trentuno**, **trentotto**; **quarantuno**, **quarantotto**, etc. Before **cento** and **mille**, **uno** is not required.

OPPOSTI *OPPOSITES*

04.04

bello	*beautiful/nice*	brutto	*ugly*
grande	*large/big*	piccolo	*small*
alto	*high/tall*	basso	*low/short*
lungo	*long*	corto	*short*
pieno	*full*	vuoto	*empty*
caldo	*hot*	freddo	*cold*
giovane	*young*	anziano	*elderly/old*
nuovo	*new*	vecchio	*old*
pesante	*heavy*	leggero	*light, weak*
fresco	*cool/fresh*	tiepido	*warm*
buono	*good*	cattivo	*bad*
dolce	*sweet*	amaro	*bitter*
pulito	*clean*	sporco	*dirty*
largo	*wide*	stretto	*narrow*
chiaro	*clear/light*	scuro	*dark*
veloce	*fast*	lento	*slow*

TIP

It's a good idea to learn words and their opposites at the same time, so making it easier to remember them both.

Dialoghi *Dialogues*

DIALOGO 1

04.05 **In this dialogue, the tea is described as bad. Why?**

Com'è questo panino?
È buono.
E il tè?
È troppo leggero e tiepido: è cattivo!

DIALOGO 2

04.06 **What's Italian coffee like?**

Com'è il caffè italiano?
Forte.

DIALOGO 3

04.07 **What is this?**

Che cos'è questo?
È un limone.

DIALOGO 4

04.08 **What are the opposites of *large* and *cold*?**

Qual è il contrario di 'grande'?
Il contrario di 'grande' è 'piccolo'.
E il contrario di 'freddo'?
'Caldo'.

04.09 **COLORI** *COLOURS*

nero	*black*
grigio	*grey*
blu	*navy blue*
azzurro	*sky blue*
viola	*purple*
verde	*green*

4 Com'è? *How is it?*   **37**

giallo	*yellow*
arancio (or arancione)	*orange*
rosso	*red*
marrone	*brown*
rosa	*pink*
bianco	*white*

> **TIP**
> **Sono** means *they are* as well as *I am* and *you are* (formal plural).

DIALOGO 5

04.10 Are there any biscuits?

C'è una birra?
No, non c'è.
Ci sono i biscotti?
No, non ci sono.

DIALOGO 6

04.11 What colour are the cars?

Di che colore è la sua automobile?
Bianca. Di che colore è la sua?
La mia è rossa.

DIALOGO 7

04.12 Does she like opera?

Le piace questa città? (*town/city*)
Sì, mi piace molto.
Le piace andare a teatro?
Sì.
Le piacciono le opere liriche? (*operas*)
Non tutte.

Language discovery

Look back at the text on bars in Italy, where we met the expression fare prima lo scontrino. What would you normally expect to see instead of lo?

1 WHERE *IL* BECOMES *LO*

To make pronunciation easier, masculine words starting with **s-** followed by a consonant (**sp**, **st**, **sv**, etc.) and words starting with **z**, **ps**, **pn** and **gn** take the article **lo** rather than **il**: **lo z_ucchero**, **lo zero**, **lo studente**. **Lo** is also used before a vowel, in which case it becomes **l'**: **l'aereo**. The plural of **lo** is **gli**: **gli spaghetti**, **gli studenti**, **gli zeri**, etc. Before such words, **un** becomes **uno**: **uno studente**, **uno zero**. **Un'** is used before feminine nouns starting with a vowel.

Remember that the main point is to successfully communicate. If you use **il** instead of **lo**, it's more than likely that nobody will even notice.

2 C'È/CI SONO *THERE IS/THERE ARE*

C'è = **ci è** *there is:* **C'è il caffè?** *Is there any coffee?* Remember that if you refer to more than one item, you need to say **ci sono**: **Ci sono le banane?** *Are there any bananas?* This refers to a specific item, e.g. the coffee or the bananas which is/are supposed to be in the cupboard. You can omit the article and say **C'è caffè? Ci sono banane?** This refers to coffee or bananas in general.

3 WEATHER AND TEMPERATURE

To say that something is cold, you say **è freddo/è fredda**; to say that the weather is cold, you say **fa freddo**. Remember that **caldo** means *hot*!

4 QUAL È…? *WHAT IS…?*

Qual è il contrario di…? (no apostrophe before the **è**). As you may already have realized, it is not always possible to translate word for word from one language into another; in the case of *What is the opposite of…?*, Italians say *Which is the opposite of…?*

5 COLOUR AGREEMENTS

Colours, like all other adjectives, need to agree with the number and gender of the noun they describe and, unlike English, they are normally placed after the noun: **un'autom_obile rossa**, **due autom_obili rosse**,

un ombrello giallo, **due ombrelli gialli**. However, **blu**, **viola**, **rosa** and **arancio** (or **arancione**) are exceptions and never change. **Verde** and **marrone** change only in the plural: **verdi**, **marroni**.

6 POSSESSION

In Italian, words such as *my, mine, your, yours, her, hers, his* and so on require the definite article (**il, la**, i, le) in front of them: **Il mio libro è qui** *My book is here*; **Dov'è il suo?** *Where is yours/his/hers?* These words are called possessive adjectives and pronouns and they must agree with the thing possessed: you say **il suo libro** *your/his/her book* because **libro** is masculine, but **la sua valigia** *your/his/her suitcase* because **valigia** is feminine.

Terms expressing family relationships, when in the singular, do not require the article.

mia madre	*my mother*	**mia moglie**	*my wife*
mio padre	*my father*	**mio marito**	*my husband*
mio fratello	*my brother*	**mio nonno**	*my grandfather*
mia sorella	*my sister*	**mia nonna**	*my grandmother*

Don't forget that, in the plural form, the article reappears: **i miei fratelli**, **le mie zie**.

7 VERBS

Here is the pattern for regular verbs of the second type:

vedere *to see*			
(io) vedo	*I see*	**(noi) vedia mo**	*we see*
(tu) vedi	*you see* (informal)	**(voi) vede te**	*you* (plural informal) *see*
(lui, lei, Lei) vede	*he, she sees, you* (formal) *see*	**(loro, Loro) vedono**	*they see, you* (plural formal) *see*

PRATICA *PRACTICE*

1 Answer the questions by choosing the correct word from the box.

Com'è questa frutta?   *Questa frutta e fresca.*

birra?   **a** Questa birra è

strada (*road*)?   **b** Questa strada è

biscotto?   **c** Questo biscotto è

caffè?   **d** Questo caffè è

gelato?   **e** Questo gelato è

dolce.   fresca.   molto.   caldo!   molto freddo!   lunga!

2 What is the opposite of…? Choose from the words in the box.

Qual è il contrario di…

a	pesante	_____
b	basso	_____
c	giovane	_____
d	corto	_____
e	vuoto	_____
f	grande	_____
g	nuovo	_____

piccolo
leggero
alto
anziano
lungo
vecchio
pieno

3 What colour is it?/What colour are they?

Di che colore è   *il latte?*   Il latte è bianco.

a	il limone?	_____
b	la banana?	_____
c	la carne? (*meat*)	_____
d	l'erba? (*grass*)	_____

Di che colore sono

e	i limoni?	_____
f	le banane?	_____

4 An Italian friend wishes to know if you have learned your numbers. Read the arithmetical expressions out loud, then write them down in full.

plus (+) = **più**   *minus (−)* **meno**

times (×) **per**   *divided by (÷)* **diviso**

$3 + 7 = 10$ Tre più sette fa (makes) dieci.

a $5 + 6 = 11$ _____
b $7 \times 10 = 70$ _____
c $1{,}000 \div 5 = 200$ _____
d $6 \times 7 = 42$ _____

5 Read these questions, fill in the replies, answering them in the affirmative, i.e. with sì (yes), then read both parts out loud. Here are two examples:

C'è il latte? Sì, c'è.

Ci sono le birre? Sì, ci sono.

a C'è il pane? _____
b C'è il caffè? _____
c C'è lo zucchero? _____
d Ci sono le banane? _____
e Ci sono i panini? _____
f Ci sono i biscotti? _____

6 Read these questions, fill in the replies, answering them in the negative, i.e. with **no**, then read both parts out loud. Here are two examples:

C'è il latte? No, non c'è.

Ci sono le birre? No, non ci sono.

a C'è il tè? _____
b C'è il vino? _____
c Cè l'acqua? _____
d Ci sono i panini? _____
e Ci sono le aranciate? _____
f Ci sono le pizze? _____

7 You are asked whether you like the various items in the list below. You don't like anything. Read these questions, fill in the replies, then read both parts out loud. (After **piace** and **piacciono**, the noun is usually preceded by an article.) Here are two examples:

Le piace la frutta? No, non mi piace.

Le piacciono i gelati? No, non mi piacciono.

a Le piace lo zucchero? _____
b Le piacciono le banane? _____
c Le piace andare al cinema? _____
d Le piace il caffè? _____
e Le piacciono i biscotti? _____
f Le piace il vino? _____
g Le piace la carne? _____
h Le piacciono le paste? _____

8 Answer the same questions as in Exercise 7. This time, you like everything, but would prefer something else. Read out loud both questions and answers.

Le piace la frutta? (gelati) Sì, mi piace ma preferisco i gelati.

a Le _____? Sì, mi _____ i biscotti.
b Le _____? Sì, mi _____ le mele (*apples*).
c Le _____? Sì, mi _____ andare a teatro.
d Le _____? Sì, mi _____ il tè.
e Le _____? Sì, mi _____ le torte (*tarts, cakes*).
f Le _____? Sì, mi _____ la birra.
g Le _____? Sì, mi _____ il pesce (*fish*).
h Le _____? Sì, mi _____ la frutta.

? Test yourself

Make up questions for the following answers:

1 Questa è una birra.

2 Sì, è buono.

3 La mia auto(mobile) è questa.

4 No, non c'è l'acqua.

5 Sì, i limoni ci sono.

6 Il mare (*sea*) è azzurro.

7 No, questo vino non mi piace.

8 No, non mi piacciono. (le mele)

9 È un panino.

10 È troppo leggero. (il tè)

SELF CHECK

I CAN. . .
. . . say what I like and dislike
. . . talk about my possessions
. . . indicate my preferences
. . . use key colours and numbers

5 Quant'è?

How much is it?

In this unit, you will learn how to:
▶ *ask for something.*
▶ *state quantities.*
▶ *ask the price.*
▶ *pronounce the names for shops.*
▶ *say numbers from 1,000 onwards.*

CEFR: (A1) *Can handle numbers, quantities and costs, and can ask people for things.*

La spesa *Shopping*

Despite the spread of supermarkets, many Italians still prefer to shop in small specialist stores where the prices may be higher but the quality of the *food* **cibo** is better and the service more personal. Traditionally, certain types of shop have the right to sell particular things, and while this is still so in some cases, it is changing. One example of this would be the *tobacconist's* **tabaccheria**, which is run by the Italian state. Here you can buy *stamps* **francobolli**, *tickets* **biglietti** for the bus, tram and train, and, bizarrely, *salt* **sale**, as it used to be a state monopoly item! One of the most endearing features of Italian life is the *newsstand* **edicola**, which is often on a street corner or in a square. Apart from *newspapers* **giornali** and *magazines* **riviste**, the **edicola** usually sells bus and local train tickets. And, don't forget, if a shop doesn't have a queuing system whereby you have to take a *number* **numerino** to be served, you might find this expression useful: **Mi dispiace ma tocca a me** *Excuse me, it's my turn!*

Look at the passage again and answer these questions in Italian:
1 If **edicola** is the word for *newsstand*, how would you say: two newsstands?
2 If **riviste** is the word for *magazines*, how would you say: one magazine?
3 If **biglietti** is the word for *tickets*, how would you say: one ticket?

Vocabulary builder

Listen to these words and expressions and then do the exercise that follows underneath.

un caffè	*one black (espresso) coffee*
un cappuccino	*one white coffee*
un francobollo per gli Stati Uniti/la Gran Bretagna	*a stamp for the USA/UK*
un chilo di mele	*a kilo of apples*
mezzo chilo di pomodori	*half a kilo of tomatoes*
un etto/cento grammi di burro	*100 grams of butter*
un litro di vino bianco	*a litre of white wine*
mezzo litro di latte	*half a litre of milk*
una scatoletta di tonno	*a tin of tuna*
una fetta di torta	*a slice of cake/tart*
un pacco di spaghetti	*a packet of spaghetti*
prosciutto (cotto)	*ham*
prosciutto crudo	*cured/parma ham*
formaggio	*cheese*
omelette (f.)	*omelette*
albicocche	*apricots*
ciliegie	*cherries*

> **TIP**
> Say...
> 1. Half a kilo of apples, please.
> 2. An espresso and two cappuccinos.
> 3. His wine is red.

SHOPPING: USEFUL PHRASES

Now listen and learn these shopkeeper expressions.

Desidera?	*Can I help you?*
Come vuole il panino?	*How do you want the roll?*
Come preferisce.	*As you prefer.*
Questi vanno bene?	*Are these OK?*
allora	*well then*
in tutto	*in all*
ecco	*here (it) is*
euro	*euro(s)*
due euro e cinque centesimi	*two euros and five cents*
il resto	*the change*
desidera altro?	*anything else?*
Deve pagare alla cassa.	*You must pay at the cash desk.*
Deve fare lo scontrino.	*You must get the receipt.*

CUSTOMER EXPRESSIONS

mi dia…	*I will have…* (lit. *give me*)
vorrei…	*I would like…*
là	*(over) there*
quelli (m.), quelle (f.)	*those*
non troppo mature	*not too ripe*
è tutto	*that's all*
Quant'è?	*How much is it?*
Quanto costa?	*How much does it cost?*
Quanto costano?	*How much do they cost?*
è troppo (caro)	*it is too much/too expensive*
è a buon mercato/costa poco	*it is cheap*
Devo telefonare.	*I must make a telephone call.*
Devo andare in banca.	*I must go to the bank.*
Devo andare a fare la spesa.	*I must go shopping.*

You will need to learn which word for *to, at* and *in* goes with each type of shop:

Vado/Sono	*I am going to/I am at (in) the…*
al supermercato	*supermarket*
al bar/*al* caffè	*bar*
al ristorante	*restaurant*
al negozio d'alimentari	*grocer's*
alla posta	*post office*
all' ufficio postale	*post office*
dal fruttivendolo	*greengrocer's*

But

Vado/Sono	*I am going to/I am at (in) the…*
in panetteria	*baker's*
in macelleria	*butcher's*
in pescheria	*fishmonger's*
in tabaccheria	*tobacconist's*
in farmacia	*chemist's*
in edicola	*newsagent's*
in libreria	*bookshop*

Note that you say **Vado/Sono**… *I am going to/I am at or in (the)*… **in piscina** *swimming pool*; **in città** *city*; **in chiesa** *church*; **in campagna** *countryside*; **in giardino** *garden*; **in ufficio** *office*; **in montagna** *mountains*; **in** or **a casa** *home*; **a letto** *bed*; **al mare** *seaside*; **a teatro** *theatre*; **al cinema** *cinema*.

In English, *to* is used to express motion towards a place (*I am going to Rome*) and *in/at* to express *being/staying* in or at a place (*I live in Milan*). In Italian, **a**, **al** and **in** depend on the noun that follows, as can be seen above.

BUYING 100 GRAMS

Un etto (short for **ettogrammo**), **due etti**, etc. means *100 grams*, *200 grams*, etc. and can be used instead of saying **cento grammi**. For *150 grams*, *250 grams*, etc., you can say **un etto e mezzo**, **due etti e mezzo**, etc., as well as **centocinquanta grammi**, **duecentocinquanta grammi**.

NUMERI DAL 1,000 IN POI *NUMBERS FROM 1,000 ONWARDS*

05.04

1.000	mille	1.000.000	un milione
2.000	duemila	2.000.000	due milioni
3.000	tremila	3.000.000	tre milioni
10.000	diecimila	10.000.000	dieci milioni
100.000	centomila	100.000.000	cento milioni
500.000	cinquecentomila	1000.000.000	mille milioni (un miliardo)

Numbers are written as one word, e.g. 977,654
novecentosettantasettemilaseicentocinquantaquattro
nine hundred (and) seventy seven thousand six hundred (and) fifty-four.

▶ **Mille** *one thousand* becomes **mila** in the plural. For example, **cinquemila**.
▶ Groups of three figures or more are separated by a dot.
▶ A comma indicates the decimal point: **1,5 uno virgola cinque** (or **uno e cinque**) *one point five.*
▶ *Eleven hundred*, *twelve hundred*, etc. are translated by **millecento** *one thousand one hundred*, **milleduecento** *one thousand two hundred.*

Dialoghi *Dialogues*

05.05 In some Italian bars, you have to pay at the cashier's desk before ordering at the counter. What does Brunella ask for?

> **TIP**
>
> It is quite common for Italians when paying for something to put the money on the counter or in a small tray, so that the vendor can see that they have given the right money.

Barista	Buongiorno, signora.
Brunella	Buongiorno. Un caffè e un panino.
Barista	Deve fare lo scontrino.
Brunella	*(to the cashier)* Un caffè e un panino, per favore.
Cassiera	Come vuole il panino? Con prosciutto, formaggio, salame, omelette…
Brunella	Ha prosciutto cotto o crudo?
Cassiera	Cotto e crudo: che cosa preferisce?
Brunella	Prosciutto crudo.
Cassiera	Va bene. Allora un caffè e un panino con prosciutto crudo. Tre e sessanta.
Brunella	*(counting the coins and giving them to the cashier)* Tre e cinquanta… tre e sessanta.
Brunella	*(to the barman)* Un caffè e un panino con prosciutto crudo. Scusi, c'è un telefono qui?
Barista	Sì, è là.
Brunella	Grazie.
Barista	Prego.

Decide whether each of these statements about Dialogue 1 is true or false:

   a She prefers cooked ham.

   b You can have a sandwich with omelette in.

   c The bar doesn't have a payphone.

DIALOGO 2

Before you listen to Dialogue 2, read it and find out how much a kilo of cherries costs.

05.06 **Francesca is buying some fruit and vegetables in the large market in the centre of Genova; first, she enquires about prices.**

Fruttivendola	Desidera?
Francesca	Quanto costano le mele?
Fruttivendola	Queste mele costano un euro al chilo; quelle uno e ottanta.
Francesca	Vorrei un chilo di queste. Le ciliege quanto costano?
Fruttivendola	Cinque euro al chilo.
Francesca	Sono troppo care. Mi dia un chilo di albicocche.
Fruttivendola	Ecco. Desidera altro, signora?
Francesca	Sì. Mezzo chilo di pomodori, non troppo maturi.
Fruttivendola	Questi vanno bene?
Francesca	Sì, grazie. È tutto. Quant'è in tutto?
Fruttivendola	Allora… le mele un euro, le albicocche tre euro, i pomodori cinquanta centesimi… Quattro e cinquanta in tutto.
Francesca	*(paying with a five-euro note)* Ecco cinque euro.
Fruttivendola	Grazie. Ecco cinquanta centesimi di resto.

 Language discovery

In Dialogue 2, how does the greengrocer distinguish between the apples nearer her and those further away? What word describes the apples nearer her and those further away?

1 QUELLO *(THAT)*

Vorrei quello/quella.	*I would like that one.*
Vorrei quelli/quelle.	*I would like those.*

Before a noun, the forms of **quello** are similar to those of the definite article (**il, lo, la, l', i, gli, le**).

quel negozio	quello scontrino	quell' aeroporto	quella chiesa
quei negozi	quegli scontrini	quegli aeroporti	quelle chiese

In Dialogue 2, the cherries cost 5 euros a kilo, in Italian literally 5 euros *to* the kilo. How would you say *2 euros a litre* litro?

2 A + IL *(TO THE)*

Vado al bar *I am going/I go to the bar*: words like **a** *to, at*, **di** *of*, **da** *from, by*, **in** *in, into* and **su** *on*, followed by a definite article (**il, lo, la**) combine as follows:

a	al	allo	alla	all'	*to the*
di	del	dello	della	dell'	*of the*
da + il	dal + lo	dallo + la	dalla + l'	dall'	*from the*
in	nel	nello	nella	nell'	*in the*
su	sul	sullo	sulla	sull'	*on the*

sul treno	*on the train*	**all'albergo**	*at the hotel*
nello studio	*in the study*	**del padre**	*of the father*
dalla stazione	*from the station*	**sulla tavola**	*on the table*

There are some 'preposition + definite article' combinations in Italian where *the* is not used in English:

all'arrivo	*on arrival*
al binario 2	*on platform 2*
alla televisione	*on television*
Vedo quel programma alla televisione.	*I watch that programme on TV.*

3 SUPERLATIVES

 When we want to emphasize the qualities of something, we use superlatives. Have a look at these typical examples and read them out out loud.

caro	**molto caro**	**carissimo**
expensive	*very expensive*	*very expensive indeed*
bello	**molto bello**	**bellissimo**
beautiful	*very beautiful*	*very beautiful indeed*
buono	**molto buono**	**buonissimo**
good	*very good*	*very good indeed*
comodo	**molto comodo**	**comodissimo**
comfortable	*very comfortable*	*very comfortable indeed*

Queste mele sono carissime.	*These apples are very expensive indeed.*
Questo caffè è buonissimo.	*This coffee is very good indeed.*
Queste scarpe sono comodissime.	*These shoes are very comfortable indeed.*

4 VERBS

Here is the pattern for regular verbs belonging to the *third type* (or conjugation).

Some **-ire** verbs take **-isc** between the stem and the ending (type IIIb), except for the first and second persons plural.

Remember that in Italian:
sc followed by an **o**, **a** or **u** is pronounced as **sk** in **sk**irt.
sc followed by an **e** or **i** is pronounced as **sh** in **sh**irt.

Type IIIa		Type IIIb	
partire	*to leave/to depart*	**finire**	*to finish*
(io) parto	*I leave*	**(io) finisco**	*I finish*
(tu) parti	*you* (informal) *leave*	**(tu) finisci**	*you* (informal) *finish*
(lui, lei, Lei) parte	*he, she leaves, you* (formal) *leave*	**(lui,lei, Lei) finisce**	*he, she finishes, you* (formal) *finish*
(noi) partiamo	*we leave*	**(noi) finiamo**	*we finish*
(voi) partite	*you* (pl. informal) *leave*	**(voi) finite**	*you* (pl. informal) *finish*
(loro, Loro) partono	*they leave, you* (pl. formal) *leave*	**(loro, Loro) finiscono**	*they finish, you* (pl. formal) *finish*

5 IRREGULAR VERBS

Some verbs do not follow the regular pattern. Here are two very important ones, both of which you have met in part before.

essere	*to be*	**avere**	*to have*
(io) sono	*I am*	**(io) ho**	*I have*
(tu) sei	*you* (informal) *are*	**(tu) hai**	*you have*
(lui, lei, Lei) è	*he, she, it is, you* (formal) *are*	**(lui, lei, Lei) ha**	*he, she, it has, you* (formal) *have*
(noi) siamo	*we are*	**(noi) abbiamo**	*we have*
(voi) siete	*you* (pl. informal) *are*	**(voi) avete**	*you* (pl. informal) *have*
(loro, Loro) sono	*they are, you* (pl. formal) *are*	**(loro, Loro) hanno**	*they have, you* (pl. formal) *have*

PRATICA *PRACTICE*

1 Ask a passer-by if nearby there is a:

   a supermarket.
   b bank.
   c chemist's.
   d tourist office.
   e bookshop.

2 Say that you:

   a must go to the bank.
   b are going to the grocer's.
   c must go to the greengrocer's.

3 Ask the greengrocer for:

   a half a kilo of ripe tomatoes.
   b five bananas.

4 Ask the shop assistant the price of:

   a 100 grams of cured ham.
   b 1 litre of milk.
   c half a litre of wine.

5 At the end of your shopping, ask how much it is in total.

6 05.07 Now listen to the recording and practise the names for these shops:

   a panetteria
   b alimentari
   c edicola
   d macelleria
   e farmacia
   f pescheria
   g ufficio postale

7 Practise reading out loud the following:

   a Un chilo di pane costa €3,20.
   b Un litro di latte costa €1,50.
   c Un etto di prosciutto crudo costa €3,40.
   d Un etto di formaggio costa €1,60.
   e Un etto di torta costa €2,50.
   f Un etto di caffè costa €1,30.

⁇ Test yourself

Write the questions for the following answers:

1 No, grazie, questo è tutto. _____
2 Due euro e cinquantotto. _____
3 Devo andare in banca. _____
4 No, non è caro: è a buon mercato. _____
5 Deve pagare alla cassa. _____
6 Vorrei un chilo di ciliege. _____
7 Tre euro e venti al chilo (pane) _____.
8 Tocca a me. _____
9 Questo prosciutto è buonissimo. _____
10 Con prosciutto e formaggio. _____

SELF CHECK

I CAN. . .
○ . . . ask the price of things in shops
○ . . . state quantities
○ . . . say the names of shops
○ . . . use numbers from 1,000 onwards
○ . . . understand prices

6 Che ore sono?
What's the time?

In this unit, you will learn how to:
▶ *tell the time.*
▶ *talk about when something is going to happen.*
▶ *say the days of the week.*
▶ *say the months of the year.*

CEFR: (A1) *Can indicate time by such phrases as next week, last Friday, in November, 3 p.m.*

Review

 Revise the following numbers, saying them out loud. If you are not sure or want to check your answers, look in the Key.

a 17	**b** 7	**c** 6	**d** 31	**e** 48
f 12	**g** 28	**h** 15	**i** 5	**j** 67
k 76	**l** 13	**m** 100	**n** 1.000	**o** 2.570
p 12.347	**q** 25.891			

Gli orari dei negozi *Shop opening hours*

Shops in Italy generally open at 8.30 a.m. and close at 12.30 p.m. for *lunch* **pranzo**. They then reopen in the *afternoon* **pomeriggio** at 3.30 p.m. and stay open until 7.30 p.m. There may be seasonal (mainly in the *summer* **in estate**), and regional differences, and in the larger *cities* **città** many shops and supermarkets don't close for lunch, operating *non-stop opening hours* **orario continuato**. On Sunday and on *public holidays* **giorni festivi**, most shops are closed. Exceptions to this are *some* **alcuni** bars and *all* **tutte** *cake shops* **pasticcerie**. There will *always* **sempre** be a *chemist's on duty* **farmacia di turno** *open* **aperta** in every town – often in or near the station.

💡 **In the text, there is the expression alcuni *some* referring to bars. If you wanted to say *some cake shops*, what would you say? Check in the Key.**

Vocabulary builder

**Look at the list of words and expressions immediately below and
then try to match up the answer to the question.**

a A che ora apre la banca? **1** E'alle tredici.
b A che ora chiude la piscina? **2** Iniziano alle venti e trenta.
c A che ora è il pranzo? **3** Chiude alle diciannove e quindici.
d A che ora iniziano i giochi? **4** Apre alle otto e mezzo.

THE TIME AND THE TIMING OF EVENTS – QUESTIONS

06.01 **Listen to these words and expressions.**

Che ore sono?/che ora è?	*What's the time?*
Sono le due e dieci.	*It's ten past two.*
alle quindici e trenta	*at half past three in the afternoon*
A che ora…	*What time…*
apre la banca?	*does the bank open?*
chiude il negozio?	*does the shop close?*
comincia/inizia il film?	*does the film start?*
finisce lo spettacolo?	*does the show end?*
aprono gli uffici?	*do the offices open?*
chiudono i musei?	*do museums close?*
finiscono di lavorare?	*do they finish work?*
è la (prima) colazione?	*is breakfast?*
è il pranzo?	*is lunch?*
è la cena?	*is dinner?*
Quando arriva l'aereo?	*When does the plane arrive?*
Quanto dura?	*How long does it last?*
Dalle sette e mezzo alle dieci.	*From seven thirty to ten.*
Dura due ore.	*It lasts two hours.*

THE TIME AND THE TIMING OF EVENTS – TIME EXPRESSIONS

06.02 **Before listening to the recording, fill in the blanks below.**

tardi/presto	*late/early*
l'altro ieri	*the day before yesterday*
ieri	*yesterday*
questa mattina (= stamattina)	*this morning*
questa sera (= stasera)	*this _____*
oggi	*today*
Che giorno è oggi?	*What day is it _____?*
domani	*tomorrow*

dopodomani	*the day after* _____
fra una settimana	*in a week's time*
più tardi	*later* (lit. more late)
mezz'ora più tardi	*half an hour* _____

Look back at the Gli orari dei negozi passage at the beginning of the unit to find the answers for the gaps below.

devo comprare…	*I must buy…*
è chiusa	*it is closed*
è aperta	*it is* _____
medicina	*medicine*
all'ora di _____	*at lunchtime*
riaprono	*(they) reopen*
dappertutto	*everywhere*
alcune _____	*some towns/cities*
ci vediamo	*we'll meet* (lit. we'll see each other); *see you (soon)*
è troppo lontano	*it's too far*
va bene	*OK*
tutti i giorni	*every day*
eccetto	*except*
anche	*also/too*

PARTI DEL GIORNO *PARTS OF THE DAY*

Before you read the list below, see if you can remember these words each with its article (il, la, lo):

a night _____
b morning _____
c evening _____

la mattina, questa mattina	*morning/in the morning, this morning*
il pomeriggio, questo pomeriggio	*afternoon/in the afternoon, this afternoon*
la sera, questa será	*evening/in the evening, this evening*

la notte, questa notte	night/at night, tonight
la notte scorsa	last night
l'alba	dawn
il tramonto	sunset

TIP
Morning also has a masculine form: **il mattino**.

I GIORNI DELLA SETTIMANA
THE DAYS OF THE WEEK

06.03 **Listen to the days of the week, pausing the recording after each one, so you can repeat it out loud. Note the accented ì at the end of the weekdays – try to make sure you do the same!**

lunedì	Monday
martedì	Tuesday
mercoledì	Wednesday
giovedì	Thursday
venerdì	Friday
sabato	Saturday
domenica	Sunday
il fine settimana/il weekend	the weekend
lunedì prossimo/scorso	next/last Monday

You may come across the word **giornata**; this describes the period of time from dawn to dusk during which something happens: **una giornata interessante** *an interesting day*, **le giornate si allungano** *the days are getting longer*. In the same way, you can say **mattinata**, **serata**, **nottata**: **una mattinata tranquilla** *a calm morning*, **una serata piacevole** *a pleasant evening*, **una nottata tempestosa** *a stormy night*. If you want to wish someone a nice day, you can say **buona giornata**.

Now unscramble the letters of the days of the week and write the correct spelling, and then match the English to the Italian.

dvoegìi _____	Saturday
codnieam _____	Friday
obatsa _____	Thursday
lìmreodce _____	Tuesday
ìnelud _____	Wednesday
rdnvìee _____	Sunday
etìmdar _____	Monday

I MESI DELL'ANNO *THE MONTHS OF THE YEAR*

gennaio	*January*	luglio	*July*
febbraio	*February*	agosto	*August*
marzo	*March*	settembre	*September*
aprile	*April*	ottobre	*October*
maggio	*May*	novembre	*November*
giugno	*June*	dicembre	*December*
il mese/il febbraio	*next/last*		
pr**o**ssimo/scorso	*month/February*		

 Look at **gennaio** and *January*. Do you notice any difference between the days of the week and months in Italian compared to English? Have a look in the Key to see if you are right!

LE QUATTRO STAGIONI *THE FOUR SEASONS*

primavera	*spring*
autunno	*autumn/fall*
estate (f)	*summer*
inverno	*winter*
l'estate pr**o**ssima/scorsa	*next/last summer*

Dialoghi *Dialogues*

DIALOGO 1

06.04 **A tourist asks a local policeman un vigile what time it is; she needs some medicine but... is she too late or too early?**

Turista	Scusi, che ore sono?
Vigile	Sono le tre e dieci.
Turista	Devo comprare una medicina ma la farmacia è chiusa.
Vigile	È troppo presto. La farmacia apre alle tre e mezzo. Deve ritornare più tardi.

06.05 **The same lady is now in the tourist office enquiring about shop opening times. At what time do they open in the afternoon? Are the opening times the same everywhere?**

Turista	Buongiorno. Quando aprono i negozi?
Signorina	La mattina?
Turista	Sì.
Signorina	La mattina aprono alle otto e mezzo.
Turista	Chiudono all'ora di pranzo?
Signorina	Sì, alle dodici e mezzo.
Turista	E il pomeriggio?
Signorina	Il pomeriggio riaprono alle tre e mezzo e chiudono alle sette e mezzo.
Turista	Questo dappertutto?
Signorina	No, in alcune città aprono e chiudono mezz'ora più tardi. Il pomeriggio, in estate, molti negozi aprono anche (*even*) alle quattro e mezzo.
Turista	Grazie. Buongiorno.
Signorina	Buongiorno.

What time do many shops reopen in the summer?

06.06 **Marina and Monica are going to the cinema. Where are they going to meet? Are they close friends?**

Monica	A che ora comincia il film?
Marina	Alle nove.
Monica	Allora ci vediamo alle nove meno un quarto?
Marina	Va bene. Dove?
Monica	Al bar Smeraldo. Va bene?
Marina	No, è troppo lontano. Puoi venire in piazza Garibaldi?
Monica	Va bene, ci vediamo in piazza Garibaldi. Ciao.
Marina	Ciao.

How do Monica and Marina say *Let's meet?* _____

# Language discovery

**In Dialogue 3, Monica and Marina plan to meet at 8.45 p.m.
If they change the appointment to le sette meno venti, what time
would they be meeting? Check your answer in the Key!**

1 TELLING THE TIME

To ask *What's the time?* you can either say **Che ore sono?** or **Che ora è?**
(lit. *What hours are they?* or *What hour is it?*). The answer will be **Sono
le…** followed by the time.

When it's **mezzogiorno** *midday*, **mezzanotte** *midnight* or **l'una** *one
o'clock*, you say **È mezzogiorno**, **È mezzanotte**, **È l'una**.

The easiest way to give the time is to say the hour followed by the
minutes. The word **minuti** is not necessary.

Sono le sette e… **cinque**, **dieci**, **quindici** or **un quarto** (*a quarter*);
venti, **venticinque**, **trenta** or **mezzo** (*half*); **trentacinque**, **quaranta**,
quarantacinque or **tre quarti** (*three-quarters*); **cinquanta**,
cinquantacinque.

When the time is from 20 minutes to the hour onwards, e.g. *twenty to
nine/a quarter to nine*, etc., you can say **Sono le nove meno venti/
Sono le nove meno un quarto**, etc. This literally means *It's nine
minus…* (*minutes*), and you will hear it used in everyday speech. Formal
announcements of time are given using the 24-hour clock.

2 DAYS OF THE WEEK

On Mondays, *on Tuesdays*, etc., is translated by **il lunedì**, **il martedì**
(**domenica** is feminine, so you say **la domenica**). For example, **Lavoro
dal lunedì al venerdì ma il sabato e la domenica non lavoro**.

3 YESTERDAY/TOMORROW

Ieri, **oggi**, **domani** and **dopodomani** never change. **Ieri**, **domani** and
dopodomani can combine with **mattina**, **pomeriggio** and **sera**; **oggi**
can combine only with **pomeriggio**, e.g. **ieri sera** *yesterday evening*,
domani mattina *tomorrow morning*, **domani pomeriggio** *tomorrow
afternoon*, **oggi pomeriggio** *this afternoon*.

4 PLURAL FORMS: *CITTÀ* AND *LOCALITÀ*

**In Dialogue 2, the signorina says alcune città *some cities*. Can you
tell if the word città is masculine or feminine?**

Like all words ending with an accented vowel, **città** and **località** do not change in the plural. For example: *one city* **una città**; *five cities* **cinque città.**

5 IRREGULAR VERBS

dovere	to have to, must	potere	to be able, can, may
devo	*I must*	**posso**	*I can*
devi	*you* (inf.) *must*	**puoi**	*you* (inf.) *can*
deve	*he, she, it, you* (formal) *must*	**può**	*he, she, it, you* (formal) *can*
dobbiamo	*we must*	**possiamo**	*we can*
dovete	*you* (pl. inf.) *must*	**potete**	*you* (pl. inf.) *can*
d̲e̲vono	*they, you* (pl. formal) *must*	**p̲o̲ssono**	*they, you* (pl. formal) *can*

Dovere and **potere** are usually followed by an infinitive, e.g. **Devo partire alle tre** *I must leave at three o'clock,* **Posso entrare?** *May I come in?*

 PRATICA *PRACTICE*

TEATRO DELLA CORTE

Via XX Settembre 20, Frascati

Tel. 589.329 581.697

Biglietteria – Orario: da lunedì a s̲a̲ bato dalle 10 alle 12:30 e dalle 15:30 alle 19. Aperture domenicali: un'ora prima dello spettacolo.
Prossimo spettacolo: **"Il nuovo inquilino"** di Eugene Ionesco. Giovedì 13 gennaio, ore 21.

---

1 Answer these questions about the Della Corte theatre.

 a Can you book at lunchtime?
 b On which day of the week can you book one hour before the show?
 c On what day and at what time can you see the next play?

2 **Answer these questions.**

   a You want to know what time the chemist's opens. How do you ask a passer-by? Remember to attract his/her attention first.

   b Can you unscramble this sentence? **A comincia che lo spettacolo ora?**

   c Provide the question for the following answer: **La mattina aprono alle otto e mezzo. _____**

3 **Assuming that today is Tuesday the 15th, how would you define the following times using one of the combinations explained in Language discovery above? For example: lunedì 14 alle 20:00 = ieri sera**

   a mercoledì 16 alle 10:30 _____

   b giovedì 17 alle 20:00 _____

   c lunedì 14 alle 09:00 _____

   d martedì 15 alle 14:30 _____

   e mercoledì 16 alle 21:00 _____

4 **Using the words in the box, complete the sentences.**

è troppo presto	quando	più tardi	chiusi	quando

   a _____ comincia il film?

   b Sono le tre. Il negozio non è aperto: _____.

   c _____ chiude il bar?

   d La farmacia è chiusa: deve ritornare _____.

   e La domenica i negozi sono _____.

? Test yourself

Give the questions to the following answers:

1 La sera i negozi chiudono alle sette e mezzo.

2 Sì, la domenica c'è sempre una farmacia aperta.

3 Nei giorni feriali, i negozi di generi alimentari restano (*stay/are*) chiusi un pomeriggio la settimana.

4 Sì, la domenica molti bar aprono.

5 No, il mercoledì pomeriggio i supermercati non chiudono.

6 Ha trenta giorni. (settembre)

7 Vado in vacanza tra (*in*) una settimana.

8 Il film finisce alle dieci e mezzo.

9 Lo spettacolo dura due ore.

10 (Oggi è) lunedì.

SELF CHECK

I CAN. . .
. . . tell the time
. . . say when something is going to happen
. . . say the days of the week
. . . say the months and seasons of the year

Review: Units 4–6

This review unit covers the main vocabulary and expressions, language skills and grammar points up to and including Units 4, 5 and 6. You can check your answers at the end of the book.

1 **Put the following words into the right column –*food* cibo, *fruit* frutta or *drinks* bevande – and add the article (il, la, l', lo, i, gli, le):**

acqua   carne   pane   latte   zucchero   pizza   tè   pasta
albicocche   gelato   limone   mele   biscotti   birra   ciliegia
arancia   spaghetti   vino   prosciutto   formaggio   burro   caffè

food cibo	*fruit* frutta	*drinks* bevande

2 **Do you know the English equivalent of the following?**
   a Devi pagare alla cassa.
   b Possiamo andare al supermercato domani?
   c Preferisco andare a teatro.
   d Vorrei due chili di questi.
   e Qual è il mio gelato?
   f Le mie scarpe (*shoes*) sono carissime.

3 **Can you remember which ending goes on these verbs?**
   a (Voi) si _____ stranieri?
   b Il film fin _____ alle undici.
   c (Loro) ved _____ il panorama.
   d Il treno part _____ alle nove.

e Le mele cost _____ 2 euro.

f I bar ha _____ un telefono?

g Scusi, (Lei) pu_____ aprire il negozio?

4 Write these numbers in words.

a 2.350

b 1.290

c 546

d 1.742.000

e 2,5

5 Look at the **scontrino** *receipt* and answer the questions below.

Bar Primula
Passeggiata a mare Camogli *via Garibaldi* *tel. 0185/770351* *Camogli (Ge)*

Quantità	Descrizione	Importo
1	Caffè	€0,80
1	Panino con prosciutto crudo	€2,80
	Totale	€3,60

a Quanto costa un caffè?

b Quanti panini mangia?

c Quant'è il totale?

6 Match these sentence halves.

a Non mi piace

b Devo comprare una medicina ma

c A che ora

d Ci sono

e Mio zio

f Oggi dobbiamo andare

g Mangio con mia madre

h In estate in Italia

i Queste albicocche

j La domenica

1 fa molto caldo.

2 finisce lo spettacolo?

3 la farmacia è chiusa.

4 sono molto care.

5 la birra.

6 all'ora di pranzo.

7 alla posta.

8 non vado in ufficio.

9 dodici mesi e quattro stagioni.

10 è dentista.

7 **Ask out loud, then write, the questions for the following answers.**

   a La banca chiude alle se dici.

   b Il contrario di **pesante** è **leggero**.

   c La mia automobile è blu.

   d Sono sei euro e cinquanta.

   e Parto alle otto.

   f Un chilo di mele costa due euro.

   g Sì, mi piace.

   h È un limone.

   i No, non mi piacciono.

   j No, non ci sono le torte.

   k Sì, abito lontano dalla stazione.

8 **Fill the spaces choosing the correct word(s) from the box below. Be careful, there are two extra ones which don't fit!**

   a Vorrei _____ a teatro stasera.

   b € 6,20 = Sei e _____ .

   c In inverno fa _____ .

   d Ci vediamo alle _____ .

   e Mi _____ gli spaghetti.

   f Gennaio è il primo _____ dell'anno.

   g Matraia è una _____ vicino a Lucca.

   h Tutti gli studenti _____ italiano.

   i Al bar devi _____ lo scontrino.

   j Questo vino è _____ !

   | fare | buonissimo | località | dieci | piacciono | mese |
   | parlano | freddo | andare | venti | piace | comprare |

9 **Translate these sentences into Italian.**

   a Do you finish work early on Friday?

   b Is the bank open today?

   c I'd like a kilo of tomatoes, please.

   d What's the opposite of *warm*?

   e You (**tu**) can go the day after tomorrow.

   f No, the museum is too far.

   g I like coffee but I prefer tea.

   h We'll meet at Bar Marisa.

   i I like living in the city.

   j We have 30 lemons.

10 Look at the drawings and answer the questions.

a Che negozio è questo?

b Che negozio è questo?

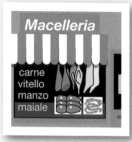

c Che cosa si compra qui?

d Che negozio è questo?

11 Answer questions a and b and translate c–h into Italian.

a Give two expressions for *post office*.

b Give the opposite of **dolce**.

c that shop/that car/this church

d those students/these umbrellas

e on arrival/on platform 4/on the table

f Via Mazzini is narrow.

g This train is very fast indeed.

h The brothers finish the beer.

12 Unscramble the words to make a sentence.

a gialla Norma e hanno automobile Federico un'.

b rosse mie comodissime scarpe sono le.

c colore tua la è automobile che di?

d ciliegie piacciono nere mi queste.

e tutti scozzesi mangiare biscotti possiamo i?

7 A che ora parte?
What time does it leave?

In this unit, you will learn how to:
▶ *ask for and understand information about trains.*
▶ *ask for single and return tickets.*
▶ *understand train announcements.*

CEFR: (A2) *Can get simple information about travel, use of public transport and can buy tickets.*

Review

1 A tourist asks you why the chemist is not open. You answer that it is too early, and that the shops open at half past three.
2 Ask a passer-by what time the shops close on a Saturday afternoon.
3 You are at the theatre: ask when the performance ends.

I treni *Trains*

Trains in Italy are distinguished by their different names, which denote their range of travel, speed and comfort. For short-distance *journeys* **viaggi** visitors to Italy are most likely to use the **regionale** or **interregionale** trains, while for longer trips the **Intercity** or the **Eurostar**. To travel on the most luxurious of these, the Eurostar, you must *book a seat* **prenotare il posto** in advance. It is the most expensive type of train. The Eurostar is the only train which does not require passengers to *validate* **convalidare** their ticket before boarding the train. For all other trains, tickets must be stamped in the small yellow machines found at the beginning and along the *platform* **binario**. Failure to do so may result in a *fine* **multa**. All types of ticket can be bought from self-service machines and at the *ticket office* **biglietteria**, while those for shorter distances, sold by the *number of kilometres* **a fascia chilom̲etrica**, are *usually* **di solito** also available in bars, tobacconists and at newsstands.

In the text, the word for *journeys* is viaggi. How do you think you say: *one journey*?

Vocabulary builder

Before you look at the list below, use what you have learned previously to translate this sentence into Italian: *What time does the train arrive?* **And then the answer:** *The train arrives at 9 a.m.*

TAKING THE TRAIN

07.01

A che ora parte?	*What time does it leave?*
il prossimo treno per...	*the next train to...*
A che ora arriva?	*What time does it arrive?*
Devo cambiare?	*Do I have to change?*
ferma a...?	*does it stop at...?*
il binario	*platform*
A che binario arriva?	*What platform does it arrive at?*
va direttamente a...?	*does it go directly to...? (a through train)*
la coincidenza	*connection*
la provenienza del treno/	*where the train*
da dove viene il treno	*comes from*
viaggiare	*to travel*
il treno è in anticipo	*the train is early*
il treno è in ritardo	*the train is late*
il treno è in orario	*the train is on time*
di solito	*usually*
vorrei sapere...	*I would like to know...*
l'orario	*timetable/schedule*
l'orario feriale	*weekly timetable*
l'orario festivo	*Sunday and holiday timetable*
il treno è in arrivo	*the train is arriving*
il treno è in partenza	*the train is leaving*
prima di	*before*
dunque	*well then*
sono sospesi	*don't run (lit. are suspended)*
Parigi	*Paris*
in ritardo	*(running) late*
in orario	*on time*

TICKETS

07.02 Look at the expressions below. Fill in the gaps, and then listen to the recording for the answers.

fare il biglietto	*to buy the/a ticket*
un biglietto di andata	*a one-way ticket*
un biglietto di _____ e ritorno	*a return/round-trip ticket*
corsa semplice	*single journey (one-way ticket)*
Per quanto tempo è valido?	*How long is it valid for?*
prima (classe)	*first class*
_____ (classe)	*second class*
_____ /riservare il posto	*to book/reserve the/a seat*
pagare il supplemento	*to pay the surcharge*
Paga la tariffa ridotta?	*Does he/she pay a reduced fare?*
obbligatorio/a	*compulsory*
facoltativo/a	*optional*
la metà	*half*
vidimare/convalidare	*to _____ (a ticket)*

Dialoghi *Dialogues*

DIALOGO 1

07.03 At the station, you overhear the following conversation between a traveller and the clerk at the ticket office. Does the train leave in the morning? Is it a direct train?

Viaggiatore	A che ora parte il prossimo treno per Firenze?
Impiegato	Alle tredici e quindici.
Viaggiatore	Va direttamente a Firenze o devo cambiare?
Impiegato	Deve cambiare a Pisa.
Viaggiatore	A che ora arriva a Pisa?
Impiegato	Alle quindici e ventinove. La coincidenza è alle quindici e cinquantacinque.
Viaggiatore	Va bene, grazie. Due biglietti per Firenze, seconda.
Impiegato	Solo andata?
Viaggiatore	Andata e ritorno. A che binario arriva?
Impiegato	Al primo binario.
Viaggiatore	Sa se il treno è in orario?
Impiegato	Non lo so. Di solito viaggia con alcuni minuti di ritardo.

Which platform will the train arrive on?

DIALOGO 2

Where is Francesca travelling to? Is she going alone?

Francesca	Buongiorno. Vorrei sapere l'orario dei treni per Como.
Impiegato	Quando vuole viaggiare?
Francesca	Domani mattina.
Impiegato	Domani è domenica: c'è l'orario festivo, alcuni treni sono sospesi. Dunque... c'è un treno che parte alle otto e cinquantasei. A Milano ha la coincidenza per Como alle dodici e nove.
Francesca	Il treno per Milano è un Intercity?
Impiegato	Sì, con prenotazione obbligatoria gratuita in prima classe e prenotazione facoltativa, a pagamento, in seconda classe.
Francesca	La bambina ha sette anni, paga la tariffa ridotta?
Impiegato	Sì, paga la metà.

 Language discovery

Look at the two expressions below. The verbs sapere and conoscere translate to exactly the same word in English. What do you think it is?

▶ Vorrei sapere l'orario dei treni per Como.
▶ Vorrei conoscere il marito di Simona.

Now look below to see how to distinguish them.

1 IRREGULAR VERBS

sapere *to know*	andare *to go*	fare *to do, make*
so	vado	faccio
sai	vai	fai
sa	va	fa
sappiamo	andiamo	facciamo
sapete	andate	fate
sanno	vanno	fanno

In Italian, there are two verbs for *to know*:

▶ **Sapere**, which is irregular, is used to express the knowledge of a fact: **So le notizie** *I know the news*, **So che Maria arriva questa sera** *I know that Maria arrives this evening*; when **sapere** is followed by an infinitive, it means *to know how to* (*to be able to*): **Angela sa guidare** *Angela can drive*.

▶ **Conoscere**, which is regular, is used to mean *to be acquainted with* (usually a person or a place): **Conosco bene Roma** *I know Rome well*; **Conosco Giacomo** *I know James*. It can also mean *to make the acquaintance of/to get to know*: **Vorrei conoscere quel pittore** *I would like to meet that artist*.

2 SPECIAL MEANINGS OF *FARE*

Fare il biglietto *to buy a ticket*. Although **fare** means *to make* or *to do*, it is used in many idiomatic phrases such as: **fare la spesa** *to go shopping*; **fare colazione** *to have breakfast*; **fare le valigie** *to pack*; **fare presto** *to be quick*; **fare benzina** *to fill up* (with petrol).

As you already know, in Italian questions are asked by simply adding a question mark at the end of the sentence, so you needn't use the verb **fare** as in English: **Che fai?** *What do you do?* **Che mangi?** *What do you eat?*

3 BISOGNA (*IT IS NECESSARY TO*)

Bisogna (= **è necessario** *it is necessary/one must*) is always followed by the infinitive of the verb:

▶ **Bisogna cambiare a Genova.**   *It is necessary to change at Genoa.*

Bisogna exists as a noun (**il bisogno** = *need, necessity*), but it is not often used.

▶ **Ho (il) bisogno di andare a Roma.**   *I (have the) need to go to Rome.*

Nowadays, it is used only as a verb (**bisognare**) and only in the third person.

4 PRONUNCIATION OF *E* AND *A*

For ease of pronunciation, when **e** (*and*) and **a** (*to*) occur before a word starting with a vowel, a **-d** is added:

▶ **Maria ed Elena vanno in vacanza.**   *Maria and Elena go on holiday.*

5 DUNQUE/ALLORA (*SO, WELL*)

Dunque *so/therefore* and **allora** *then* are frequently used in Italian at the beginning of a sentence and, as with the English *well*, they have no particular meaning.

1 **Select the correct answers from the box to complete the dialogue.**

no, prima   sì, ecco   andata e ritorno   domani mattina

Impiegato	Quando desidera viaggiare?
Viaggiatore	_____ .
Impiegato	Solo andata?
Viaggiatore	_____ .
Impiegato	Seconda classe?
Viaggiatore	_____ .
Impiegato	Sei e sessantacinque. Ha quindici centesimi?
Viaggiatore	_____ .
Impiegato	Grazie. Ecco tre e cinquanta di resto.

2 07.05 **First, read the sentences and the exercise, then listen to the announcements on the recording, and choose the right answer for each one (allontanarsi** *to go away***, (in this context)** *to keep at a distance***).**

Treno regionale per Genova delle ore sedici e trentacinque viaggia con venti minuti di ritardo.

Treno espresso da Roma per Losanna è in arrivo al binario quattro.

Attenzione. Attenzione. Treno Eurocity da Roma per Parigi è in transito al binario due. Allontanarsi dalla linea gialla.

a Il treno per Genova   ferma in tutte le stazioni.
                           non ferma in tutte
                           le stazioni.
                           è in orario.

b Il treno espresso   va a Roma.
                           va a Losanna.
                           ha quattro minuti
                           di ritardo.

c L'Eurocity   ferma a Genova.
                           ferma a Parigi.
                           è in anticipo.

3 Unscramble these sentences.

a un Roma ritorno andata di per biglietto e _____

b treno binario che a arriva da il Genova? _____

c due valido il è biglietto mesi per _____

d a parte ora che l' Firenze per Intercity? _____

e festivo sapere vorrei l'orario _____

f direttamente cambiare va o devo? _____

g ritardo di minuti alcuni treno il viaggia con _____

4 Play the part of the man (**Impiegato**) at the ticket office. Go through the dialogue and prepare your answers. Fill in the gaps, then read the whole conversation out loud.

Viaggiatore	Scusi, a che ora parte il prossimo treno per Roma?
Impiegato	(*The next train to Rome leaves at 10:02.*) _____
Viaggiatore	Va direttamente a Roma o bisogna cambiare?
Impiegato	(*It is necessary to change at Padova.*) _____
Viaggiatore	A che ora è la coincidenza?
Impiegato	(*The connection is at 11:00, and you arrive in Rome at 18:30.*) _____
Viaggiatore	È un treno interregionale?
Impiegato	(*No, it is an Intercity train.*) _____
Viaggiatore	Bisogna prenotare il posto?
Impiegato	(*Yes, it is necessary to book the seat.*) _____
Viaggiatore	Allora un biglietto per Roma, per favore.
Impiegato	(*Single?*) _____
Viaggiatore	Per quanto tempo è valido il biglietto?
Impiegato	(*Two months.*) _____
Viaggiatore	Allora andata e ritorno.
Impiegato	(*First or second class?*) _____
Viaggiatore	Seconda.

⁇ Test yourself

This is part of an Italian railway timetable. Study it carefully, and answer the *true* **vero** or *false* **falso** questions below about one of the trains. These symbols will help you:

EC	«EuroCity» – Treni di qualità in servizio internazionale diurno.
IC	«InterCity».
iR	Treno «interregionale».
R	Treno «regionale» con divieto di fumare.
Ⓡ	Prenotazione obbligatoria.
R	Prenotazione facoltativa.
Ⓐ	Si effettua nei giorni lavorativi escluso il sabato.
Ⓑ	Si effettua tutti i giorni escluso il sabato.
✗	Treno con servizio di ristoro in carrozza ristorante del tipo tradizionale.

1 Lei (*you*) è alla stazione di Genova P. Principe alle due e trenta del pomeriggio e deve essere a Savona per (*by*) le tre e trenta del pomeriggio. Lei deve prendere il treno delle 14.55.

2 Il treno è un regionale.

3 Bisogna prenotare.

4 Il treno viene da Venezia.

5 C' è questo treno il sabato.

6 Questo treno fa servizio ristorante.

SELF CHECK

I CAN...	
●	... ask for train information and understand the reply
●	... understand the difference between **conoscere** and **sapere**
●	... ask for a train ticket
●	... understand station announcements

8 Che cosa vuoi fare oggi? *What do you want to do today?*

In this unit, you will learn how to:
▶ *say what you want to do.*
▶ *understand and ask for advice.*
▶ *make comparisons.*

CEFR: (A2) *Can make arrangements to meet, decide where to go and what to do. Can also use simple descriptive language to make brief statements about and compare objects and possessions.*

 Review

You are at the station *information office* **ufficio informazioni**. The *clerk* **impiegato** tells you that the train is running 20 minutes late. You then ask on which platform it will arrive, and he tells you it will arrive on platform 7. Fill in the gaps and say the conversation out loud.

Impiegato	Sì _____ con _____ _____ _____ _____ .
You	A _____ _____ arriva?
Impiegato	_____ al _____ _____ .

La passeggiata *The stroll*

The stroll **passeggiata** is an important part of Italian city and village life. It is focused on the *main street* **corso** and usually takes place in the late afternoon before *dinner* **cena**, and may involve having an **aperitivo** along the way. *In summer* **in estate**, when it is more pleasant to be *outside* **all 'aperto**, people might take an evening stroll, perhaps to enjoy an *ice cream* **gelato** or a delicious *water ice* **granita**. The **passeggiata** is an opportunity *to meet* **incontrare** friends, to chat and to see and be seen, and definitely should be experienced!

Knowing that passeggiata is a noun, can you work out what the verb for *to stroll* is? Look in the Key for the answer.

Vocabulary builder

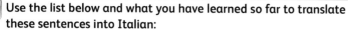

Use the list below and what you have learned so far to translate these sentences into Italian:

1 I would like to go to the cinema.
2 I want to go to the countryside.
3 I prefer to stay at home.

The same form of verb follows all of them: *I would like, I want to, I prefer.*
What is it? Check the Key for the answer!

OPINIONS, PREFERENCES AND RECOMMENDATIONS

08.01 **Listen to these expressions.**

Voglio…	*I want…*
stare a casa	*to stay at home*
guardare la televisione	*to watch television*
vedere la partita	*to see the match*
andare a teatro	*to go to the theatre*
Ne voglio tre.	*I want three (of them).*
Ne voglio alcuni.	*I want some (of them).*
Preferisco uscire.	*I prefer to go out.*
secondo me	*in my opinion*
pensare	*to think*
Quale mi consiglia?	*Which one do you recommend?*
Che cosa mi consiglia?	*What do you recommend?*
per vedere	*to see*
due posti	*two seats*
li prendo?	*Shall I take them?*
abbastanza interessante	*quite interesting*

COMPARISONS AND OTHER USEFUL VOCABULARY

08.02 **The letters of these words have been jumbled up. Can you find them in the vocabulary list that follows? Then listen to the recording.**

1 ranaco _____
2 oparcemr _____
3 ermnet _____

costa di più	*it costs more*
le opere d'arte più interessanti	*the most interesting works of art*
adesso	*now*
poi	*then/after that*
compleanno	*birthday*
comprare un regalo	*to buy a present*
non lo ha ancora	*he/she doesn't have it yet*
mentre	*while*
vita	*life*
piano	*floor/storey*
pensa che	*(just) think*
palazzo	*building*
l'ascensore non funziona mai	*the lift/elevator never works*
ne abbiamo molte	*we have many (of them)*
quest'altra	*this (other) one*
spiega in dettaglio	*it explains in detail*
prezzo	*price*

> **TIP**
>
> **Volta** means *time*: **una volta, due volte, tre volte** *once, twice, three times* etc.

NUMERI ORDINALI *ORDINAL NUMBERS*

1st **primo**	*5th* **quinto**	*9th* **nono**
2nd **secondo**	*6th* **sesto**	*10th* **decimo**
3rd **terzo**	*7th* **settimo**	*11th* **undicesimo**
4th **quarto**	*8th* **ottavo**	*12th* **dodicesimo**

From 11th onwards, ordinal numbers are formed by dropping the final vowel of cardinal numbers and adding **-esimo** at the end (except in the case of **-tre** – **ventitreesimo**, **trentatreesimo**, etc. – which retain the vowel). As the ordinal numbers are adjectives, their endings need to agree with the noun they qualify.

| **la *prima* volta** | *the first time* |
| **al *terzo* piano** | *on the third floor* |

With dates, ordinal numbers are used only with the first day of the month; for other dates, the simple cardinal number is used.

| **il primo luglio** | *the first of July* |
| **il due agosto** | *the second of August* |

Dialoghi *Dialogues*

08.03 **Since Sergio and Francesca are married, they use the tu form when speaking to each other. Today is Saturday. What are they planning to do?**

Sergio	Che cosa vuoi fare oggi?
Francesca	Adesso devo andare al supermercato, poi voglio andare in libreria a comprare un regalo per il compleanno di Chiara.
Sergio	Che cosa pensi di comprare?
Francesca	Mah, non so, forse l'ultimo libro di Umberto Eco: so che non lo ha ancora.
Sergio	Puoi comprare alcune penne biro per me? Le vorrei rosse.
Francesca	Va bene, mentre sono in centro voglio andare al teatro Margherita a vedere se ci sono due posti per questa sera: c'è Aida. Se ci sono li prendo?
Sergio	Va bene, se hanno i biglietti andiamo all'opera ma se non li hanno possiamo andare al cinema: c'è un film sulla vita di Mozart che voglio vedere.
Francesca	Tu, dove vai?
Sergio	Io devo andare da Paolo per un consiglio riguardo al lavoro. Pensa che abita al sesto piano in un palazzo dove l'ascensore non funziona mai!

Decide if these statements are true or false.

a Sergio needs some blue pens.
b Francesca is going to the supermarket first.
c Paolo lives on the seventh floor.

08.04 **While Francesca is in the bookshop, she decides to buy a guidebook on the most artistic Italian cities. Does she buy the smaller or larger book?**

Francesca	Ha una guida illustrata delle città italiane?
Libraio	Ne abbiamo molte, signora.
Francesca	Ne vorrei una non troppo cara ma interessante. Lei che cosa mi consiglia?
Libraio	Secondo me queste due sono le migliori: questa costa di meno perché ha le fotografie in bianco e nero ma è abbastanza interessante; quest'altra ha molte illustrazioni a colori e spiega in dettaglio le opere d'arte più interessanti; costa di più ma è più completa.
Francesca	Quella grande mi piace di più: la prendo.

Language discovery

In the last line of Dialogue 1, Francesca says la prendo. What does la refer to? Why is it in the feminine gender? Check the answer in the Key to see if you are right!

1 HIM, HER, IT AND THEM

Lo, **la**, **li**, **le**: these words translate *him*, *her*, *it* and *them*.

Vedo Mario.	**Lo** vedo.	I see Mario.	I see him.
Mangio la frutta.	**La** mangio.	I eat fruit.	I eat it.
Leggo i libri.	**Li** leggo.	I read the books.	I read them.
Compro le penne.	**Le** compro.	I buy the pens.	I buy them.

As you can see from the examples above, **la**, **lo**, **li** and **le** go before the verb and not after, as in English (literally *him I see*, *it I eat*, etc.).

Lo and **la** followed by a word starting with a vowel or **h-** can take an apostrophe: **l'amo** or **lo amo/la amo** *I love him/her*. **Li** and **le** do not change.

2 TALKING ABOUT THE FUTURE

 In Dialogue 1, Francesca asks Sergio Li prendo? She is talking about the future, but what tense is she using? Look below to check your answer.

Li prendo? *Shall I get them?* In spoken Italian, when referring to the future, the present tense is widely used.

Domani vado al cinema.	*Tomorrow, I am going to the cinema.*
L'estate prossima andiamo in vacanza alle Bahamas.	*Next summer, we are going on holiday to the Bahamas.*

3 OF THEM/OF IT

Ne abbiamo molte *We have many of them.* **Ne** stands for *of them/of it.*
It is used with expressions of quantity or with numerals. In English, the
corresponding words are often omitted.

Quanto prosciutto vuole?	*How much ham do you want?*
Ne voglio due etti.	*I want 200 grams (of it).*
Ha bambini?	*Do you have any children?*
Sì, ne ho due.	*Yes, I have two (of them).*

4 COMPARISONS

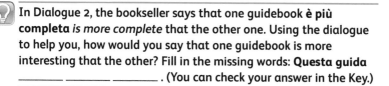

In Dialogue 2, the bookseller says that one guidebook **è più
completa** *is more complete* that the other one. Using the dialogue
to help you, how would you say that one guidebook is more
interesting that the other? Fill in the missing words: **Questa guida
_____ _____ _____ .** (You can check your answer in the Key.)

In English, there are two ways to say *more* and *most*: with short words, *-er* or
-est are added (*rich, richer, richest*) and with longer words, *more* or *most* are
used (*intelligent, more intelligent, the most intelligent*). Italian always uses
più for *more* and **più** preceded by the definite article (**il, la, i, le**) for *most*.

Questa borsa è grande.	*This bag/purse is big.*
Questa borsa è più grande.	*This bag/purse is bigger.*
Questa borsa è la più grande.	*This bag/purse is the biggest.*

Meno, besides *minus,* means *less* and is used in the same way as **più.**

Questa casa è grande.	*This house is big.*
Questa casa è meno grande.	*This house is less big (smaller).*
Questa casa è la meno grande.	*This house is the least big (smallest).*

At the end of a phrase, **di più** or (**di**) **meno** are used.

Lui lavora di più.	*He works more.*
Voglio spendere (di) meno.	*I want to spend less.*

Note: with **meno**, **di** can be omitted.

Di (or **di** + article) are used to translate *than*.

Roberto è più giovane di Carlo.	*Roberto is younger than Carlo.*
Il pane costa meno della carne.	*Bread costs less than meat.*

5 IRREGULAR ADJECTIVES AND ADVERBS

Note the following irregular adjectives and adverbs (adverbs are words which describe a verb).

buono	**migliore**	**il migliore**
good	*better*	*the best*
bene	**meglio**	**il meglio**
well	*better*	*the best*
cattivo	**peggiore**	**il peggiore**
bad	*worse*	*the worst*
male	**peggio**	**il peggio**
badly	*worse*	*the worst*

Remember the agreement of the two adjectives above: **buono/a/i/e** and **cattivo/a/i/e**.

 Add the right endings onto the adjectives in these sentences:

  a La bistecca è buon _____ ma il pesce è migliore. *The steak is good, but the fish is better.*

  b Pierino è cattiv _____ ma suo fratello è peggiore. *Pierino is bad, but his brother is worse.*

A note on andare

Andare *to go* can be used with many different expressions, e.g. **Andare...**

a fare una passeggiata	*for a walk*
a fare la spesa	*shopping*
al cinema	*to the cinema/movies*
al mare	*to the seaside*
in ufficio	*to the office*
in campagna	*to the countryside*
in montagna	*to the mountains*
in città	*to town*
da Giuliana	*to Giuliana's house*
dal dentista	*to the dentist*
dal meccanico	*to the garage*

6 IRREGULAR VERBS

volere *to want*	stare *to stay/to remain*
voglio	sto
vuoi	stai
vuole	sta
vogliamo	stiamo
volete	state
vogliono	stanno

TIP
As with **potere** and **dovere**, **volere** is also usually followed by an infinitive.

 PRATICA *PRACTICE*

1 A group of Italian teenagers meet in a café and discuss how to spend the afternoon.

  a Sara wants to go for a walk.
  b Bruno prefers to go to the cinema.
  c Giovanni wants to go to the seaside.
  d Franco prefers to stay in town.
  e Barbara, who does not like any of the proposed activities, says she wants to go home!

Make up a dialogue:

  a Sara   Io _____
  b Bruno   Io _____
  c Giovanni   Io _____
  d Franco   Io _____
  e Barbara   Io _____

2 Using the information in Exercise 1, say and write what the five teenagers want to do.

  a *Sara vuole andare a fare una passeggiata.*
  b _____.
  c _____.
  d _____.
  e _____.

3 Choose a verb from the first column, add a word from the second column and then one from the third to make a meaningful sentence. You should be able to create at least five. Here's an example: *Preferisco uscire domani.*

Voglio		vedere		domani
Posso		guardare		a casa
Preferisco	+	andare	+	Maria
Devo		uscire		a Roma
		stare		la televisione

4 Answer these questions using the first person singular and **ne**.

a Quanti panini vuole? (*three*) Ne voglio tre.
b Quante automobili ha? (*one*) _____ .
c Quanti ne prende? (*eight*) _____ .
d Quanto formaggio vuole? (*100 grams*) _____ .
e Quanti anni ha? (*28*) _____ .
f Quante valigie ha? (*two*) _____ .

5 Using the words in the box, complete the following sentences (**sta male** *is not well*).

a Questo vino è buono ma quello è _____ .
b Marta sta male ma io sto _____ .
c Questo programma è cattivo ma l'altro è _____ .
d Il film mi piace ma il libro mi piace _____ .
e Questa guida è più piccola: costa _____ .

(di) meno   di più   peggiore   migliore   peggio

6 This receipt records the purchase of four books. Using the Italian words for expensive, more expensive and least expensive fill in the gaps.

a Il libro che costa €12,00 è _____ ma quello da €20,00 è _____ _____ .
b I due libri da €10,00 e €8,00 sono i _____ _____ .

* LIBRERIA DRUETTO *	
PIAZZA C.L.N. 223 TO	
P . IVA 00484520010	
D03	20,00
D03	10,00
D03	12,00
D02	8,00
	50,00 TL
37	16–05–03
//=BA	6226353

⑦ Test yourself

You are buying some wine. How do you say the following to the shop assistant?

1 Which is the best?

2 Which one do you recommend?

3 I don't want a sweet wine.

4 I want to spend less.

5 I prefer this one.

6 I want three litres (of it).

Now give the Italian equivalent of the following:

7 The large bag is better.

8 Meat costs more than bread.

9 I speak well, but you speak better.

10 The most interesting works of art are in Florence.

SELF CHECK

I CAN...
○ ... give my intentions
○ ... compare things
○ ... ask for advice and understand the reply
○ ... talk about the future

Quando si alza?
When do you get up?

In this unit, you will learn how to:
▶ *talk about the things you do every day.*
▶ *say how often something happens.*

CEFR: (A2) *Can ask and answer questions about habits and routines.*

Review

Translate these sentences into Italian:
1 The day after tomorrow I'm seeing Carlo.
2 Roberto talks more than Silvia.
3 We sell many of them. (*apples*)

 # Viaggiare su strada *Travelling by road*

Italy has a wide network of *motorways* **autostrade**, most of which charge a *toll* **pedaggio**. All *tollbooths* **caselli** accept *credit cards* **carte di credito** for anyone without any *cash* **contanti**. For those who want *to hire* **noleggiare** *a car* **macchina**, remember that on motorways and outside urban areas, it is compulsory to have *dipped headlights* **fari anabbaglianti**, even *during the day* **anche di giorno**. If you are visiting between late autumn and early spring, in most of the country you must have *snow chains* **catene** *on board* **a bordo**.

As an alternative to trains, there are many long-distance *coaches* **pullman**, which connect the major cities and *airports* **aeroporti**. As on urban *buses* **autobus**, passengers are normally expected to buy their ticket *before boarding* **prima di salire**; however, there are exceptions to this, such as buses to airports. On most types of bus, you will have to validate your ticket on board.

 In the text above, look at the words for *coaches* and *buses*. What is unusual about them? Look in the Key for the answer.

Vocabulary builder

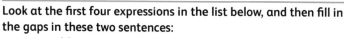

Look at the first four expressions in the list below, and then fill in the gaps in these two sentences:

_____ addormento tardi.

_____ diverte tantissimo.

Try to translate them into English, and then check your answers in the Key.

HABITS AND ROUTINES

09.01

Mi sveglio presto.	*I wake up early.*
Mi alzo alle sette.	*I get up at seven.*
Mi lavo tutti i giorni.	*I wash every day.*
Si veste da sola.	*She gets (herself) dressed.*
sempre	*always*
Vado sempre in campagna.	*I always go away to the country(side).*
mai	*never/ever*
Non vado mai al cinema.	*I never go to the cinema.*
Prendo l'autobus.	*I take the bus.*
Vado in macchina.	*I go by car.*
salire	*to board*
scendere	*to get off (a bus, train etc.)*
anche di giorno/notte	*even during the day/night*
spesso	*often*
Vado spesso a teatro.	*I often go to the theatre.*
qualche volta	*sometimes*
Qualche volta esco.	*I sometimes go out.*
Altre volte sto a casa.	*At other times, I stay at home.*
Non fumo più.	*I don't smoke any more.*
Come lo passate?	*How do you spend it?*
Facciamo una passeggiata.	*We take a stroll/go for a walk.*
Voi fumate ancora?	*Do you still smoke?*
abbastanza presto	*fairly early*
Ne porto una tazza a…	*I take a cup (of it) to…*
Prepariamo la colazione.	*We get breakfast ready.*
Facciamo colazione tutti insieme.	*We have breakfast all together.*

OTHER USEFUL VOCABULARY

Read down the whole list, and then match up the Italian with the English:

a	C'è qualcosa di interessante.	**1**	*There is nothing interesting.*
b	C'è qualcuno.	**2**	*Is anybody there?*
c	C'è nessuno?	**3**	*I don't know anybody.*
d	Non c'è nessuno.	**4**	*Nobody comes.*
e	Non viene nessuno.	**5**	*There is something interesting.*
f	Non conosco nessuno.	**6**	*There is someone.*
g	Non c'è niente d'interessante.	**7**	*There is never anything interesting.*
h	Non c'è mai niente d'interessante.	**8**	*There is nobody.*

 09.02

qualche cosa/qualcosa	*something*
qualcuno	*someone/somebody*
nessuno	*no one/nobody*
anche	*even*
intera	*whole*
tutti e tre	*the three of us (of them)*
oppure	*or*
al massimo	*at the most*
cucina	*kitchen*
certo	*sure, of course*
adesso è abbastanza grande	*now she is big enough*
verso le otto	*at about eight*
genitore (m)	*parent*
godere di	*to enjoy*

Dialoghi *Dialogues*

DIALOGO 1

09.03 **Michela has just arrived to spend a few days at Sergio and Francesca's, and she enquires how they pass their time. How often do they watch television?**

Michela	La sera uscite spesso o state a casa?
Francesca	Qualche volta usciamo per due o tre sere consecutive, altre volte stiamo a casa anche una settimana intera. Questo la sera, perché di giorno naturalmente usciamo.
Michela	E il fine settimana, come lo passate?
Sergio	Dipende. Se mia sorella ci viene a trovare, oppure vengono i genitori di Francesca, stiamo a casa o, al massimo, facciamo una passeggiata. Se non viene nessuno andiamo quasi sempre tutti e tre in campagna. Qualche volta vengono anche i miei amici o le amiche di Francesca.
Michela	Guardate mai la televisione?
Francesca	Generalmente no. Soltanto qualche volta, se c'è qualcosa di estremamente interessante.
Michela	(*lighting a cigarette*) Voi fumate ancora?
Sergio	No, non fumiamo più.

a Do Francesca and Sergio go out every night?

b Were Francesca and Sergio smokers before?

c Find the expression meaning 'all three of us'.

09.04 **Michela asks how they start their day. What time does Francesca get up?**

Michela	La mattina a che ora vi svegliate?
Sergio	Ci svegliamo abbastanza presto: io mi sveglio alle sei e mezzo, mi alzo, vado in cucina a fare il caffè e ne porto una tazza a Francesca. Poi mi lavo, mi faccio la barba e mi vesto.
Michela	E tu Francesca, a che ora ti alzi?
Francesca	Io mi alzo alle sette meno un quarto; mi lavo, mi vesto, mi pettino e poi sveglio Valentina.
Michela	Valentina si veste da sola?
Sergio	Certo: adesso è abbastanza grande. Noi due prepariamo la colazione, e Valentina si veste; poi facciamo colazione tutti insieme. Poi, verso le otto, usciamo.

Decide if these statements are true or false.

a Once he gets up, Sergio immediately washes.

b Valentina is the last one to get up.

c Valentina isn't able to get dressed by herself.

Language discovery

Using what you learned in Dialogues 1 and 2 about routines and negatives, fill in the gaps in the sentences below. Alessandra is describing the morning routine of her partner, Umberto. (You can check your answers in the Key.)

Non _____ alziamo _____ prima delle sette. Poi Umberto, il mio compagno, _____ fa la barba, e _____ veste. Beve un caffè e poi esce. Non mangia _____ (*two possibilities*) al mattino.

1 REFLEXIVE VERBS

Io lavo la camicia *I wash the shirt*: in this phrase, **io** is the subject, **lavo** the verb, and **la camicia** is the object; the action expressed by the verb is carried out by the subject on the object.

However, in some cases, verbs can express an action which 'reflects' back to the subject: in **Io mi lavo** *I wash myself*, the action of washing refers back to the subject (*myself*); in this case, the verb *to wash oneself* is called a reflexive verb.

Myself, *himself*, *herself*, etc. are called reflexive pronouns and in most cases, unlike in English, are placed before the verb. *To wash oneself* is formed by replacing the final **-e** of the verb **lavare** *to wash* with **-si:** thus **lavarsi** *to wash oneself*.

lavarsi *to wash oneself*		
(io)	**mi lavo**	*I wash (myself)*
(tu)	**ti lavi**	*you wash (yourself)*
(lui, lei, Lei)	**si lava**	*he/she washes (him/herself), you* (formal) *wash (yourself)*
(noi)	**ci laviamo**	*we wash (ourselves)*
(voi)	**vi lavate**	*you wash (yourselves)*
(loro, Loro)	**si lavano**	*they wash (themselves), you* (pl. formal) *wash (yourselves)*

When a reflexive verb is in the infinitive form, its final **-si** is removed and the pronoun is attached to it.

Voglio lavarmi.   *I want to wash (myself).*

Devo alzarmi.   *I must get (myself) up.*

Some verbs are reflexive in both English and Italian.

divertirsi   *to amuse/enjoy oneself*

farsi male   *to hurt oneself*

radersi/farsi la barba   *to shave (oneself)*

The English verbal form *to get* + past participle or adjective usually corresponds to an Italian reflexive verb.

abituarsi (a)   *to get used (to)*

stancarsi   *to get tired*

Si also translates *one/you* in phrases like:

Si vede la differenza.   *One/you can see the difference.*

Si prende l'autobus.   *One takes/you take the bus.*

Here are some common Italian reflexive verbs.

svegliarsi	*to wake up*
alzarsi	*to get up*
vestirsi	*to get dressed*
pettinarsi	*to comb (one's hair)*
svestirsi	*to get undressed*
addormentarsi	*to fall asleep*
accorgersi	*to realize*
scusarsi	*to apologize (for)*
sbagliarsi	*to be mistaken*
sedersi	*to sit down*

2 PERSONAL PRONOUNS: *MI, TI, CI, VI*

 In Dialogue 1 (09.03), Francesca says: Se mia sorella ci viene a trovare. What does ci mean here?

Besides translating *myself*, etc., these words can also mean *me, you* and *us*.

Mi vedi?	*Can you see me?*
Ti telefono domani.	*I'll phone you tomorrow.*
Ci scrive spesso.	*He/She often writes to us.*
Vi faccio vedere la strada.	*I'll show you* (plural) *the road.*

3 IRREGULAR VERBS

uscire *to go/come out*	venire *to come*
esco	vengo
esci	vieni
esce	viene
usciamo	veniamo
uscite	venite
escono	vengono

4 DOUBLE NEGATIVE

In English, with negative words like *never*, *nothing* and *nobody/no one*, *not* is omitted. However in Italian, it is retained and the double negative is used.

Non compro niente.   *I don't buy anything* (lit. *I don't buy nothing*).

Non parla mai.   *He/she never speaks.*

Non vede nessuno.   *He/she doesn't see anybody.*

5 PRESTO/IN ANTICIPO *EARLY*

Note the difference between these two expressions:

Mi alzo presto.   *I get up early.*

Il treno arriva in anticipo.   *The train arrives early.*

Presto can mean *early*, *soon* and *quickly*. **In anticipo** is used when referring to something which happens before a specific (scheduled) time.

6 PLURALS

TIP

In Italian, **p-** followed by **s** or **n** is pronounced (unlike English, where it is silent).

In order to keep the sound of the **c** and the **g** hard, most nouns ending in **-co**, **-ca**, **-go** and **-ga** form their plurals with **-chi**, **-che**, **-ghi** and **-ghe** respectively.

il pacco	*parcel*	**i pacchi**	*parcels*
la banca	*bank*	**le banche**	*banks*
il fungo	*mushroom*	**i funghi**	*mushrooms*
il dialogo	*dialogue*	**i dialoghi**	*dialogues*

However, a few masculine nouns are exceptions to this rule and form their plurals with **-ci**.

l'amico	*friend*	**gli amici**	*friends*
il medico	*doctor*	**i medici**	*doctors*
lo psicologo	*psychologist*	**gli psicologi**	*psychologists*

PRATICA *PRACTICE*

1 09.05 **Sergio and Francesca are paying you a visit. They propose that you should address each other with the tu form – Diamoci del tu! – and you accept: D'accordo. You then ask Francesca about herself. Follow the recording, saying the questions in Italian. Write them in, and then check your answers in the Key.**

You	*What time do you wake up in the morning?* _____
Francesca	Io mi sveglio verso le sei e mezzo.
You	*And at what time do you get up?* _____
Francesca	Mi alzo verso le sette meno un quarto.
You	*What time do you go out?* _____
Francesca	Esco alle otto.
You	*Do you go out by yourself?* _____
Francesca	No, esco con Sergio e Valentina.
You	*Do you have breakfast together?* _____
Francesca	Sì, insieme.

2 09.06 **Now ask Sergio about himself.**

You	*Who prepares breakfast?* _____
Sergio	La prepariamo insieme.
You	*Does Valentina have breakfast with you?*
Translate:	_____
Sergio	Sì.
You	*Valentina goes out with you: isn't that too early for her?*
	_____
Sergio	No, perchè in Italia la scuola inizia alle otto e mezzo.

3 Fill in the gaps.

a Sergio si _____ .

b Si _____ .

c Si _____ .

d Si _____ .

e Fa _____ con Francesca e Valentina.

f Poi _____ tutti insieme.

4 **Fill the spaces using the words below.**

  a Vado _____ in ufficio, eccetto il sabato e la domenica.
  b Non vado _____ al cinema.
  c Vado _____ a teatro.
  d _____ volta vado in campagna, _____ volte sto a casa.
  e C'è _____?
  f Non c'è _____.
  g Spesso alla televisione non c'è _____ d'interessante.
  h Quando vado a teatro c'è sempre _____ che ha la tosse (*cough*).

qualcuno   niente   spesso

sempre   nessuno   nessuno

qualche   altre   mai

5 **Write in the answers in Italian, and read them out loud. Check your answers in the Key.**

  a You are in a mountain village and you enter a shop, but the shop assistant seems to be missing. What do you say? _____
  b Later, you are asked if you know anybody in the village: say you don't. _____
  c You then meet a local carrying a basket full of lovely mushrooms. Ask if she often goes mushrooming (**andare per funghi**). _____
  d Ask her if she ever goes to town. _____

1   Little Marco is a naughty boy: there are things that he never does, others he does all the time. Make sentences from each pair of words in this way, using sempre *always* and mai *never:*

alzar si tardi   lavar

sempre   mai

Si alza sempre tardi e non si lava mai.

a addormentarsi   stancarsi
b vestirsi male   pettinarsi
c parlare   ascoltare (*to listen*)
d guardare la televisione   lavorare
e divertirsi   studiare
f sapere tutto   ubbidire (*to obey*)
g mangiare dolci   lavarsi i denti

2   Give the plural of the following.
a pacco
b amico
c banca
d psicologo
e parco
f alga
g mucca

SELF CHECK

I CAN. . .
● ...talk about the frequency of things
● ...explain routine habits
● ...use the most common reflexive verbs
● ...form a double negative

10 Ha prenotato?
Did you book?

In this unit, you will learn how to:
▶ *talk about things that happened at a definite point in the past.*

CEFR: (A2) *Can ask and answer questions about pastimes and past activities.*

Review

Fill in the missing words in these sentences:

1 Grazia e Tommaso _____ svegliano _____ otto meno un quarto.
2 Non conosco _____ in questa città, però _____ una passeggiata in centro.
3 Laura e le sue ami _____ _____ sempre la sera, e vanno in discoteca.

Documenti *Documents*

According to Italian *law* **legge** (f.), all citizens and visitors must always have a form of photo ID on their person. Italians have an *identity card* **carta d'identità** while foreign nationals should keep their *passport* **passaporto** or other recognized form of *document* **documento** with them. From the finest *hotel* **albergo** to the simplest *youth hostel* **ostello per la gioventù**, all visitors must show valid ID before they can *check in* **fare il check-in**.

This law applies also to anyone driving in Italy. If the *police* **carabinieri** stop you, they will want to see not only your ID but also a current *driving licence* **patente**.

The same is true even in Internet cafés, where valid ID is necessary before you can go **online**. The best rule of thumb is *to keep* **tenere** your documents with you *at all times* **in ogni momento**. Hotels and other forms of *lodging* **alloggio** should give your document back to you almost *immediately* **subito**, although this is not always respected. A gentle reminder should do the trick!

 How would you say in Italian *many laws*? Check in the Key for the answer.

Vocabulary builder

First, look at this list of expressions to do with events in the past and fill in the gaps – they are all words you have met before. Then listen to the recording.

10.01 VERBS TAKING *ESSERE* IN THE PAST TENSE

Sono partito/a _____.	*I left early.*
Sono arrivato/a _____.	*I arrived late.*
Sono uscito/a subito.	*I went out at once.*
Sono entrato/a nel _____.	*I entered the shop.*
Sono ritornato/a a _____.	*I returned home.*
Sono salito/a sull'autobus.	*I got on the bus.*
Sono sceso/a dall'autobus.	*I got off the bus.*
è ritornata da…	*he/she has returned from…*

10.02 VERBS TAKING *AVERE* IN THE PAST TENSE

Ha prenotato?	*Have you* (formal) *booked?/Did you* (formal) *book?*
Ho prenotato/riservato…	*I have booked/reserved…*
due posti/un tavolo/una camera	*two seats/a table/a room*
Ho confermato la prenotazione.	*I have confirmed the booking.*
Ho perso _____ treno.	*I have missed the train.*
Ho perso il _____.	*I have lost the ticket.*
Ho finito il denaro/i soldi.	*I have spent/used up the money.*
Non ho cambiato la valuta.	*I have not changed (the) any money.*
Ho dimenticato i _____.	*I have forgotten the passports.*
Ho mangiato _____.	*I have eaten enough.*
Ho pagato il conto.	*I have paid the bill/check.*
Ho viaggiato molto.	*I have travelled a lot.*
Ho telefonato alla polizia.	*I have phoned the police.*
ha detto	*he/she said*
ha visto	*he/she saw*

10.03 OTHER USEFUL VOCABULARY

come al solito	*as usual*
così	*so*
con calma	*calmly*
a proposito	*by the way*
senti!/senta!	*listen!* informal/formal (both often used)
la settimana scorsa	*last week*
varie cose	*various things*
fare un prelevamento (= prelevare)	*to withdraw (money)*
ritirare	*to collect, pick up (a thing)*
per salutarti	*to say hello to you*
per te	*for you*
hai mangiato	*you have eaten*
già	*already*
Egitto	*Egypt*
l'aereo	*aeroplane*
dormire	*to sleep*
vaso	*vase*
guasto/a	*out of order, not working*

Dialoghi *Dialogues*

DIALOGO 1

10.04 **Sergio and Francesca are organizing themselves for their trip to Paris the next day. Can you say in Italian when Francesca confirmed the hotel booking?**

Sergio	Ho riservato un tavolo da Manuelina per questa sera, così non abbiamo il problema di cucinare e possiamo preparare le valige con calma. A proposito, hai confermato la prenotazione all'albergo di Parigi?
Francesca	Sì, ho confermato la settimana scorsa. Senti, ieri ho comprato varie cose e ho finito i soldi: puoi andare in banca a fare un prelevamento?
Sergio	Certamente. Hai ritirato gli assegni turistici?
Francesca	Sì, ieri. Allora ci vediamo stasera. Buon lavoro!
Sergio	Buon lavoro anche a te. Ciao.

a Sergio is going to the bank to get the traveller's cheques. True or false?

10.05 The three of them have now arrived at Manuelina's. Is their table inside or outside?

Cameriere	Ah, i signori Ferrari! Buonasera. Hanno riservato?
Sergio	Sì, un tavolo per tre.
Cameriere	(*checking the booking*) Hanno un tavolo riservato in veranda, come al solito. Va bene?
Sergio	Benissimo, grazie.
Cameriere	S'accomodino.

DIALOGO 3

10.06 They order their meal, then Sergio tells Francesca that her friend Manuela, who has just arrived back from her holiday, was on the phone earlier. Did Manuela go to the museum?

Sergio	Oggi ha telefonato Manuela per salutarti: è ritornata dall'Egitto; ha detto che ritelefona più tardi.
Francesca	Quando è arrivata?
Sergio	Ieri sera. Ha detto che l'aereo è partito con due ore di ritardo così è arrivata a Genova tardissimo ed è andata subito a dormire.
Francesca	Sai se è stata al museo del Cairo? (*to Valentina*) Valentina, mangia più lentamente!
Sergio	No, non ha parlato del museo. Ha detto che ha visto dei bellissimi vasi e ne ha comprato uno per te.
Valentina	Mamma, posso prendere un altro gelato?
Francesca	No, Valentina, hai già mangiato troppo.

Answer these questions and check the answers in the Key.

4a How late was Manuela's flight in leaving?

b What has Manuela bought for Francesca?

c Why isn't Valentina allowed another ice cream?

Language discovery

In Dialogue 3, Sergio talks about Manuela's return from her holiday in Egypt. He says that: ...*è ritornata* dall'Egitto *she came/has come back from Egypt* and *ha detto* che ritelefona più tardi *she said that she will call back later.* Look at the two verbs *in italics*; can you work out an important rule concerning verbs which take **essere** in the past tense? Check the Key for the answer!

1 PAST PARTICIPLE AND PERFECT TENSE

To talk about the past in simple everyday situations, e.g. **Ho prenotato una camera**, Italians use the present tense of **avere** followed by what is known as the past participle. This forms the perfect tense. The past participle is formed by replacing the verb endings **-are**, **-ere** and **-ire** with **-ato**, **-uto** and **-ito** respectively.

Infinitive		Past participle	
cenare	*to dine*	cenato	*dined*
avere	*to have*	avuto	*had*
spedire	*to send*	spedito	*sent*

Ieri ho cenato a casa.   *I dined at home yesterday.*

Maria ha avuto l'influenza.   *Maria has had the flu.*

Ho appena spedito il pacco.   *I've just sent the parcel.*

This form is used to express both something one has done and something one did.

Some past participles have a form of their own (an irregular form). The most common are:

aprire	*to open*	aperto	*opened*
chiudere	*to close/shut*	chiuso	*closed/shut*
dare	*to give*	dato	*given*
essere	*to be*	stato	*been*
dire	*to tell*	detto	*told*
fare	*to do/to make*	fatto	*done/made*
leggere	*to read*	letto	*read*
perdere	*to lose/miss*	perso	*lost*
prendere	*to take*	preso	*taken*
scendere	*to go/come down*	sceso	*gone/come down*
stare	*to stay*	stato	*stayed*
vedere	*to see*	visto	*seen*

2 VERBS TAKING *ESSERE*

Some verbs of state (e.g. **essere** *to be*, **stare** *to stay*) or motion (e.g. **andare** *to go*, **arrivare** *to arrive*) and all reflexive verbs take **essere** rather than **avere**.

> **TIP**
> As you can see in the above list of verbs, the past participle of **essere** is borrowed from the verb **stare**.

sono andato	*I went/I have gone*
sono partito	*I left/I have left*
mi sono lavato	*I washed (myself)/I have washed (myself)*

NB: These verbs must agree in number and gender with the subject.

> **TIP**
> Note that **camminare** *to walk*, despite being a verb of motion, takes **avere**. For example: **Ho camminato per tre chilometri**. *I walked for three kilometres.*

Roberto è arrivato.	*Roberto arrived/has arrived.*
Manuela è partita.	*Manuela left/has left.*
Il medico e il notaio sono venuti.	*The doctor and the notary came/have come.*
La bambina e la suora sono partite.	*The girl and the nun left/have left.*

3 MORE PREPOSITIONS

Ai, **dai**, **sui**, etc. In Unit 5, you saw how the prepositions **a**, **di**, **da**, **in** and **su** combine with **il**, **lo** and **la**; the same prepositions combine with **i**, **gli** and **le** in a similar way.

a	= ai	= agli	= alle
di	= dei	= degli	= delle
da + i	= dai + gli	= dagli + le	= dalle
in	= nei	= negli	= nelle
su	= sui	= sugli	= sulle

dalle loro case	*from their homes*
sugli autobus	*on the buses*
sui treni	*on the trains*
nelle banche	*in the banks*

Del, **dello**, **della**, **dei**, **degli**, **delle** are also used to express *some*.

Vorrei delle fragole.	*I'd like some strawberries.*
Ha dello zucchero?	*Have you got some sugar?*

Mangia più lentamente! Words which qualify (illustrate) the verb (**cammino lentamente** *I walk slowly*) are called adverbs. In English, they are normally formed by adding *-ly* to the adjective: *slow – slowly*; in Italian, **-mente** is added to the feminine form, e.g. **onesto** (m.), **onesta** (f.).

onesto	*honest*	**onestamente**	*honestly*
rapido	*quick*	**rapidamente**	*quickly/ rapidly*

Adjectives ending in **-le** and **-re** drop the final **-e** before adding **-mente**.

facile	*easy*	**facilmente**	*easily*
difficile	*difficult*	**difficilmente**	*with difficulty*

PRATICA *PRACTICE*

1 **While in Italy, you write a diary about your stay. First you jot down in Italian a list of your movements. You…**

a got up early. _____

b had breakfast at 7.30. _____

c read an Italian newspaper. _____

d called *a taxi* (**un tassì**). _____

e went to the museum. _____

f left the museum. _____

g went to the bank. _____

h returned to the hotel. _____

TIP
Remember to make the agreement with your gender when using **essere**.

2 **There has been a burglary in the apartment next to where Sergio and Francesca live. The police ask questions of all the residents. Change the verbs in the chart into the past tense and use them to complete the following dialogue. You will need to use some verbs more than once.**

svegliarsi	fare	andare	vestirsi
alzarsi	portare	lavarsi	svegliare

Poliziotto   La mattina a che ora vi siete svegliati?

Sergio   Ci siamo _____ abbastanza presto: io mi _____

_____ alle sei e _____ _____ in cucina a fare il

caffè, e ne _____ _____ una tazza a Francesca. Poi mi

_____ _____, mi sono fatto la barba e mi _____

_____.

Poliziotto   E Lei, signora, a che ora si è alzata?

Francesca   Io mi _____ _____ alle sette meno un quarto;

mi _____ _____, mi _____ _____ e poi

_____ _____ Valentina. Dopo colazione siamo usciti.

Poliziotto   Hanno sentito dei rumori insoliti?

Francesca   No, assolutamente niente.

Sergio   Devo dire di no, tutto normalissimo.

You are camping at Viareggio. There is a couple next to your tent. The lady, having realized that you are not Italian, comes to welcome you. First, read out the dialogue, trying to say the answers in Italian. Then write the answers and read the dialogue out out loud again.

Signora   Buongiorno. Loro non sono italiani...

You   *Tell her no, you are English.* _____

Signora   Quando sono arrivati?

You   *Say we arrived this morning.* _____

Signora   Ma Lei parla italiano perfettamente! Viene qui ogni anno?

You   *Say no, this is the first time* (volta). _____

Signora   Noi veniamo qui ogni anno perchè questa è una zona molto

tranquilla.

You   *Ask her where is she from.* _____

Signora	Io sono di Milano ma mio marito è toscano, per questa ragione veniamo qui in Toscana.
You	*Tell her you have been in Florence for a week.* _____
Signora	Firenze! È certamente molto bella ma in questa stagione fa troppo caldo in città!
You	*Say yes, it is too hot there, so you have decided (deciso di) to come here.* _____
Signora	Sa che Lei è veramente molto simpatica (really very nice)? Perchè questa sera non vengono a cenare (to dine) con noi? Io mi chiamo Liliana...

4 **Fill the gaps with the right adverb, forming it from the words in the box, remembering to drop the final -e or to change the adjective into the feminine form before adding -mente. For example: (veloce) Franco ha velocemente chiuso la porta.**

normale   possibile   chiaro   terribile   diretto   speciale   lento

a Mi piace la birra _____ quella inglese.
b Bisogna mangiare _____ .
c _____ bisogna prenotare.
d Vorrei partire _____ domani.
e Questo treno va _____ a Roma.
f Questo ombrello è _____ caro.
g Per farsi capire bisogna parlare _____.

 10.07 **Listen to the passage and write down what you hear. Then check your spelling in the text below.**

L'abitazione *Housing*

La maggior parte degli italiani che abitano in città vive in appartamenti in palazzi a molti piani. Gli edifici (*buildings*) moderni hanno naturalmente un ascensore ma molti edifici vecchi non lo hanno, quindi (*therefore*) ogni giorno, spesso più volte al giorno, i residenti devono salire e scendere molte scale (*stairs*). Forse però (*however*), questo è un bene (*a good thing*) perchè per molte persone che vivono in città questo è il solo esercizio fisico che fanno! Circa il ventisei per cento degli italiani possiede una seconda casa al mare, in montagna o in campagna e quando possono vanno là a passare il fine settimana e le vacanze. Recentemente però il governo ha aumentato (*increased*) la tassa (*tax*) sulla seconda casa e naturalmente molti proprietari sono scontenti.

? Test yourself

1 **Look again at the passage on the previous page, and use it to help you answer these questions in Italian.**

a Dove vive la maggior parte degli italiani che <u>a</u>bitano in città?

b C'è l'ascensore in tutti i palazzi?

c Quali sono gli edifici che non hanno l'ascensore?

d Molte persone che v<u>i</u>vono in città fanno molto esercizio fisico?

e Quanti italiani poss<u>ie</u>dono una seconda casa?

f Dove si trova la seconda casa?

g Quando vanno nella loro seconda casa?

h Che d<u>e</u>vono fare ogni giorno i residenti senza ascensore?

i Che cosa ha fatto recentemente il governo?

j I proprietari delle seconde case sono contenti?

2 **Can you find the mistakes in these sentences? Write the correct versions. Be careful, there may be more than one mistake in each sentence!**

a Delia ha presa l'autobus alle otto.

b Dario e Mauro sono partito ieri per treno.

c La macchina viaggia troppo rapidomente.

d Valentina mangia tanto ciliegie.

e I carabinieri si hanno alzato molto presto.

SELF CHECK

I CAN...
● ... talk about events in the past
● ... describe how something is done
● ... understand a text written entirely in Italian

 Review: Units 7–10

This review unit covers the main vocabulary and expressions, language skills and grammar points up to and including Units 7, 8, 9 and 10. You can check your answers at the end of the book.

1 You are buying a ticket at the railway station in Bologna. Say each sentence out loud in Italian, then write it down.

You	Good morning, I'd like a ticket for the next train to Venice (Venezia).
Impiegato	The next train is a Eurostar. Is that OK?
You	Is it more expensive than the other trains?
Impiegato	Yes, but it is quicker.
You	OK. What time does it leave?
Impiegato	At 9.37. First or second class?
You	Second. Thank you. Do I have to validate the ticket?
Impiegato	No, not Eurostar tickets.
You	Good. Which platform does it arrive at?
Impiegato	Platform 7. Have a good day.
You	Thank you. You too.

2 Fill in the missing words. Choose from lo/la/l'/li/le/ne.

  a Hai i biglietti? Sì, _____ ho.

  b Tiziana compra il giornale tutti i giorni? Sì, _____ compra sempre.

  c Mangi questa mela dopo pranzo? Sì, _____ mangio.

  d Vedi le tue amiche domani? Sì, _____ vedo ogni sabato.

  e Giulia e Corrado hanno tanti CD? No, non _____ hanno molte.

  f Ci sono dei posti liberi? Sì, ce _____ sono due in carrozza (*carriage*) quattro.

  g Volete delle fragole? _____ abbiamo già, grazie.

  h Hai visto Franco ieri? No, _____ ho visto la settimana scorsa.

i Il signor Bargioli ti ha dato le fotografie oggi?	No, me _____ dà dopodomani.
j Avete perso l'autobus?	Sì, _____ abbiamo perso.

3 **Write these dates in Italian.**
   a The fourth of December.
   b The first of May.
   c The seventeenth of October.
   d The twenty-sixth of June.

4 **Read the text and fill in the missing words from the list below.**

Leonardo e Lucrezia lavorano _____ notte. Allora, _____ alzano alle cinque del pomeriggio. Lucrezia _____ lava prima di lui. Poi Leonardo si _____ la barba mentre Lucrezia _____ veste. _____ colazione insieme, e _____ di casa alle otto di sera. _____ a lavorare alle dieci, e _____ alle sei del mattino. Tornano a casa, fanno la cena, e _____ addormentano alle nove del mattino.

si   si   fanno   escono   si   iniziano   di   fà   si   finiscono

5 **Do you know the English equivalent of the following?**
   a Ho mangiato benissimo.
   b Vi siete conosciuti in Spagna?
   c Abbiamo fatto una passeggiata nel parco.
   d Signora, vuole sedersi?
   e Non esco mai dopo mezzanotte.
   f La mia macchina è migliore di quella di Luca.
   g Di solito il pullman arriva in ritardo.
   h La settimana prossima vado in campagna.
   i Ne prendo due, tre volte al giorno.
   j Quando compro una rivista, la leggo subito.

6 **Look at all the things that Francesca did the day she went on holiday. Make sentences from the prompts.**
   a alzarsi alle sei
   b farsi la doccia (to shower)
   c lavarsi i denti
   d vestirsi velocemente
   e preparare il caffè
   f fare (la) colazione
   g chiamare un tassì
   h uscire di casa
   i andare alla stazione

j comprare un biglietto in seconda classe

k prendere il treno per Napoli

l noleggiare una macchina

m andare alla villa di sua sorella a Positano

n cenare con sua sorella

o addormentarsi presto

7 **Read this passage and answer the true (T) or false (F) questions below it.**

LE REGIONI *THE REGIONS*

L'Italia è formata da venti regioni che godono di un certo grado di autonomia dal governo centrale. Cinque di queste regioni hanno uno statuto speciale che dà loro una maggiore (più grande) autonomia; queste sono: Sicilia, Sardegna, Friuli Venezia-Giulia, Trentino-Alto Adige e Valle d'Aosta. Quest'ultime (latter) sono bilingue: italiano-tedesco per il Trentino Alto-Adige e italiano-francese per la Valle d'Aosta. Prima dell'unificazione dell'Italia (1861) ogni regione era (was) uno stato indipendente o parte di qualche altro stato europeo e per questa ragione ogni regione aveva (had), e ancora ha, dialetti che possono differire grandemente l'uno dall'altro e dalla lingua standard.

Questi dialetti si riflettono nella pronuncia della lingua ufficiale. Anche le tradizioni, i costumi e la cucina differiscono grandemente da regione a regione. L'avvento della televisione negli anni cinquanta e la migrazione interna hanno promosso un processo di standardizzazione che è ancora in atto. Il fatto che tutte le città italiane più importanti sono state (were) le capitali della loro regione spiega la loro enorme ricchezza artistica.

Vero *true* **o falso** *false*?

a Ci sono cinque regioni bilingue.

b Il francese è parlato in Valle d'Aosta.

c L'Italia è stata creata nel 1861.

d Le regioni non hanno più dialetti.

e La televisione è stata importante nella standardizzazione della lingua italiana.

8 **Look for the mistakes in these sentences (there may be more than one in each sentence!).**

a Si svegliamo alle sette meno uno quarto.

b Gaia dice: So Elena molto bene – siamo andato a scuola insieme.

c Ugo ha molto animali, ma preferisce i gatti.

d Milena parla molto del sport.

e Le bambine si sono pettinati per due ore!

f Perchè venite mai a trovarci a Toscana?

g Oggi ho visto il film per la terzo volta.

9 **Put the correct form of the prepositions (a, di, da, in, su) in the gaps.**

a Vorrei andare _____ cinema.

b Ho parlato _____ miei problemi.

c Filippo è sceso _____ treno.

d I residenti sono usciti _____ loro case quando hanno sentito l'allarme.

e Vedo sempre la partita (*match*) _____ spalti (*terraces*).

f È un amico _____ miei genitori.

g Maria ed Angela sono salite _____ pullman _____ ultimo momento.

h Mi sono seduto _____ banco _____ giardino.

i Abbiamo detto _____ nostri amici che non possono venire.

j Sei stata due ore _____ dentista?

10 **Translate the following sentences into Italian.**

a My bag is bigger.

b Eleonora is younger than Giampaolo.

c This restaurant is the best in Siena.

d She speaks French very badly.

e The cheese is bad but the cake is worse.

f That book is more interesting than this one.

g Thank you. My brother is very well.

h Fish costs more than meat.

i Clara is less tired than Samantha.

j My Italian is good but my Portuguese is better.

11 **Ask out loud, then write, the questions for the following answers.**

a Mi alzo quando mi sveglio.

b Bisogna cambiare a Pisa.

c Stamattina devo portare i pacchi alla posta.

d Voglio viaggiare domani sera.

e Ne ho due – Arturo, ventidue anni, e Belinda, diciannove.

f Quest'estate andiamo in Cina.

g Sì, hai bisogno del tuo passaporto.

h Sì, mi sono sbagliata.

i No, non voglio sapere il risultato.

j Arriva al binario 9.

La spesa
Shopping

In this unit, you will:
▶ *practise shopping for food and clothes.*
▶ *practise asking for a discount.*
▶ *revise numbers (Units 3, 4, 5).*
▶ *revise how to ask for something, how to state quantities, how to ask the price (Unit 5).*
▶ *revise how to describe something (Unit 4).*

CEFR: (A2) *Can deal with common aspects of everyday living such as shopping, and can make simple purchases by stating what is wanted and asking the price.*

Il cibo in Italia *Food in Italy*

Agli italiani piace mangiare bene. Molti vanno ogni giorno a fare la spesa al mercato dove comprano cibi genuini a prezzi ragionevoli. Molte persone hanno una vera (*true*) mania per i cibi genuini e durante il fine settimana vanno in campagna a comprare carne di animali non trattati (*treated*) con antibiotici, verdure coltivate senza pesticidi e vino fatto senza additivi. Il cibo è considerato un interessante argomento (*topic*) di conversazione. Anche la televisione spesso trasmette programmi dedicati alla buona cucina (*cuisine*). Ogni regione italiana offre specialità gastronomiche locali e spesso in paesi e villaggi si organizzano feste e, nella piazza principale, si offrono gratis – o a prezzi minimi – squisiti piatti di specialità locali. Tra le priorità di molti italiani c'è anche l'abbigliamento (*clothes*) e l'arredamento (*furnishings*) delle loro case.

HA CAPITO? *HAVE YOU UNDERSTOOD?*

1 **Che cosa vanno a comprare in campagna molti italiani?**

2 **Parlano spesso di cibo?**

3 **Oltre all'arredamento ed al cibo che cosa è importante per molti?**

Cibo/cibi/vivande *Food*

11.01

una porzione di…	*a portion of…*
vitello arrosto	*roast veal*
pollo arrosto	*roast chicken*
verdure ripiene	*stuffed vegetables*
una fetta di torta di verdura	*a slice of vegetable pie*
salame nostrano	*locally produced salami*
una scatoletta di pomodori pelati	*a tin of peeled tomatoes*
una lattina di…	*a can of…*
caffè macinato	*ground coffee*
birra	*beer*
Coca-Cola	*Coca-Cola*
una bottiglia di olio di oliva (or: d'olio d'oliva)	*a bottle of olive oil*
mezza dozzina di uova	*half a dozen eggs*
un pezzo di formaggio	*a piece of cheese*
che tipi ha?	*what kinds do you have?*
un cespo di lattuga	*a head of lettuce*
un pacchetto/una confezione di piselli surgelati	*a packet/bag of frozen peas*
un grappolo d'uva	*a bunch of grapes*
carne macinata	*minced meat/ground beef*
salsiccia/manzo	*sausage/beef*
maiale/agnello	*pork/lamb*
pesce (*m.*)	*fish*
burro	*butter*
(pomodori) pelati	*peeled tomatoes*
una pagnotta integrale	*a wholemeal loaf*
Questo pesce è fresco?	*Is this fish fresh?*
grasso	*fat*
stagionato	*fully matured*

assaggiare	*to taste*
pecorino	*sheep's milk cheese*
piccante	*strong*
uova di giornata	*freshly laid eggs*
Lo può incartare?	*Can you wrap it?*
Può mettere tutto in un sacchetto/una busta?	*Can you put everything in a (carrier) bag?*
grazie lo stesso	*thanks all the same*
tra	*between, among*
voglio dire	*I mean*
Un po' caro, no?	*A bit dear/expensive, isn't it?*

TIP

One way of helping you remember these new words is to think about them when doing your own shopping. Try to imagine that you have to order everything you need in Italian.

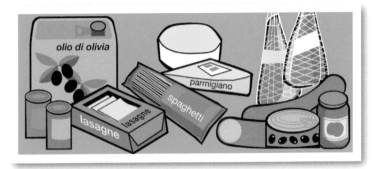

CEREALI INTEGRALI *WHOLEGRAIN CEREALS*

Study the advertisement and answer the questions below.

Meglio integrale, ma...

Nella parte esterna dei cereali integrali (quella che normalmente si elimina con la raffinazione) si trovano la fibra, le vitamine, i sali minerali e persino un antibiotico naturale.

Purtroppo è proprio su questa parte esterna che si concentrano inevitabilmente i pesticidi e le sostanze chimiche usate normalmente in agricoltura.

1 In what part of the grain is most of the goodness found?

2 What else may be found there?

3 What is the advertisement proposing?

Dialoghi *Dialogues*

11.02 **Oggi Manuela non ha il tempo per cucinare (*the time to cook*) e va in rosticceria. Quali sono gli ingredienti delle verdure ripiene?**

Manuela	Due porzioni di vitello arrosto e una fetta di torta di carciofi (*artichokes*).
Rosticcere	La fetta va bene così, o la vuole più grande?
Manuela	Così va bene. Questo che cos' è?
Rosticcere	Queste sono zucchine (*courgettes*) ripiene.
Manuela	Voglio dire… che ripieno è?
Rosticcere	Uova, carne, formaggio, funghi, origano…
Manuela	Me ne dia una porzione.
Rosticcere	Desidera altro?
Manuela	Per oggi è tutto, grazie. Quant'è?
Rosticcere	Undici e trentasei in tutto.

Language discovery

Me ne dia una porzione. Before **ne**, **lo**, **la**, **li** and **le**, these pronouns:

mi	ti	ci	si	vi	become
me	te	ce	se	ve	

Reading the following Italian sentences out loud several times, keeping in mind their meaning, will be beneficial to your progress.

Mi ha dato il libro. **Me lo ha dato.**	*He/she gave me the book.* *He/she gave it to me.*
Ti dò un biscotto. **Te lo dò.**	*I'll give you a biscuit.* *I'll give it to you.*
Ci ha portato una birra. **Ce l'ha portata.**	*He/she brought us a beer.* *He/she brought it to us.*
Ne vuole di più?	*Do you want more (of it)?*
No, me ne dia un po' (di) meno.	*No, give me a little less (of it).*

PRATICA 1

It's your turn now. Make up this dialogue with the **rosticcere**.

You	*What filling is it?*
Rosticcere	Tonno e maionese.
You	*You will take two portions of it. Then you would like one portion of roast chicken and one of fish salad. Is the fish salad fresh?*
Rosticcere	Freschissima.
You	*Ask if he can wrap it well and how much it is.*
Rosticcere	Sette e sessantanove.
You	*Here are ten euros.*
Rosticcere	Ecco due e trentuno di resto.

DIALOGO 2

11.03 Francesca è in campagna con la sua famiglia e va a fare la spesa nel villaggio. Che tipo di caffè compra? Che tipo di uova vuole?

Francesca	Vorrei del salame nostrano non troppo grasso.
Negoziante	Ho questo stagionato, buonissimo. Lo vuole assaggiare?
Francesca	Sì, grazie. Mmm… è buono, me ne dia tre etti. Mi dia anche un pezzo di pecorino non troppo piccante.
Negoziante	Va bene così, o ne vuole di meno?
Francesca	Così va bene. Vorrei anche una scatoletta di tonno e una lattina di caffè macinato. Che tipi ha?
Negoziante	Ne abbiamo molti tipi ma il Lavazza Oro è il migliore.
Francesca	Va bene. Mi dia anche una dozzina di uova di giornata. Può mettere tutto in un sacchetto?

Say that you would like:

  a 300 grams of ham, not too fatty

  b six cans of beer

  c a piece of cheese, not too strong

  d half a dozen freshly laid eggs

  e a tin/packet of ground coffee

  f a packet of frozen peas

  g a tin of peeled tomatoes

  h 200 grams of butter

DIALOGO 3

Adesso Francesca va dal fruttivendolo. Perchè i pomodori costano cari?

Francesca	Quanto costano i pomodori oggi?
Fruttivendolo	Due e sessantacinque al chilo.
Francesca	Un po'cari, no?
Fruttivendolo	Questi sono pomodori nostrani freschissimi, signora.
Francesca	Me ne dia mezzo chilo. Poi vorrei tre grappoli d'uva bianca ed un cespo di lattuga.
Fruttivendolo	Nient'altro, signora?
Francesca	Un chilo di pesche (*peaches*). Mi dia anche un po' di verdura per fare il minestrone.
Fruttivendolo	Le patate (*potatoes*) e le cipolle (*onions*) le ha?
Francesca	Sì. Ho anche i fagioli (*beans*).
Fruttivendolo	Allora … un po' di fagiolini (*green beans*), due zucchini, carote, un porro (*leek*), e una fetta di zucca (*pumpkin*).
Francesca	Va bene. È tutto per oggi. Quant'è?
Fruttivendolo	Dunque… i pomodori, l'uva, la lattuga, le pesche, la verdura per il minestrone… Nove euro in tutto.

Language discovery

UN PO'

Un po' cari, no?: **po'** is the shortened form of **poco** *little*. **No?** or **non è vero?** at the end of a sentence corresponds to the English *isn't it?, aren't you?, don't they?*, etc.

TIP
1 The plural form of **l'uovo** (masculine) is irregular: **le uova** (feminine and ending with **-a**). 2 **La zucchina**, **le zucchine** also has a masculine form: **lo zucchino**, **gli zucchini**.

Remember that **po'** takes an apostrophe and not an accent, as one often encounters in emails, text messages and the like.

PRATICA 3

Answer these questions:

a You have no vegetables at home and you want to make a good minestrone. What do you buy?

b Ask for one bunch of black grapes.

c Ask the greengrocer if the green beans are local.

d Say that you would like half a pumpkin.

e Say that it is all for today.

f You are in the **panetteria**; ask for half a kilo of wholemeal rolls.

g Tell the **pescivendolo** that this fish is not fresh, you don't want it.

PRATICA 4

Read the following passage and answer the questions below.

In rosticceria e in panetteria *Takeaway food*

Nelle rosticcerie si può comprare cibo pronto da asporto (*to take away*): porzioni di pollo e vitello arrosto, torte di verdura, insalate di pesce e tante altre specialità nazionali e locali. Le panetterie vendono molti tipi di pane, grissini (*breadsticks*) e focacce (*flat loaves*): focacce con cipolla, salvia (*sage*), olive o fatte con la farina (*flour*) di granturco (*maize*), fette di pizza, biscotti, eccetera. Il formaggio parmigiano fresco è eccellente da mangiare a piccoli pezzi con l'aperitivo oppure alla fine del pasto (*meal*). La vera mozzarella napoletana è fatta con latte di bufala ma al giorno d'oggi (*nowadays*) spesso è fatta con latte di mucca (*cow*).

Vero o falso? *True or false?*

a Nelle rosticcerie si possono comprare gli ingredienti per fare la pizza.

b La vera mozzarella è fatta con latte di mucca.

c Il parmigiano è buono con l'aperitivo.

Abbigliamento *Clothes*

Che taglia ha?	*What size do you take?*
Che numero ha?	*What size (shoes) do you take?*
Mi fa uno sconto?	*Can you give me a discount?*
in vetrina	*in the shop window*
camerino	*fitting room*
camicia/camicetta	*shirt/blouse*
gonna	*skirt*
maglia	*jumper/sweater*
maglietta	*T-shirt*
cintura	*belt*
abito/vestito	*dress or suit*
collant	*tights/pantyhose*
un paio di…	*a pair of…*
scarpe/pantaloni/jeans	*shoes/trousers, pants/jeans*
sciarpa di seta/lana	*silk/wool scarf*
borsa di pelle	*leather bag*
modello	*style*
svendita	*sale*
stretto/a	*tight, narrow*

DIALOGO 4

11.05 **Francesca e Chiara vanno in un grande magazzino department store. Che cosa comprano?**

Chiara	Ha questo vestito nella taglia 42, in giallo?
Commessa	La 42 in giallo no. Li abbiamo in verde, blu e nero. In giallo abbiamo altri modelli.
Chiara	Allora no. Queste magliette quanto costano?
Commessa	Soltanto sette e settantacinque: sono in svendita.
Chiara	Allora ne prendo due: una nera e una rosa.
(meanwhile)	
Francesca	Queste scarpe quanto costano?
Commessa	Cento euro.
Francesca	Le posso provare?
Commessa	Certo. Che numero ha?
Francesca	Il 38. Le vorrei blu.
Commessa	In blu abbiamo il 371/2 o il 39.
Francesca	*(trying them on)* Ummm… queste sono un po' strette e queste sono troppo lunghe. Grazie lo stesso.

11.06 **You are in a shoe shop. Listen and follow the instructions on the recording. The complete the dialogue by filling in the missing words. The answers are in the Key.**

Taglie *Clothing sizes*									
Women's coats, suits, dresses and blouses	Britannica	10	12	14	16	18	20		
	Americana	8	10	12	14	16	18		
	Continentale	38	40	42	44	⑯	48		
Adults' shoes	Britannica	4	5	6	7	8	9	10	11
	Americana	5½	6½	7½	8½	9½	10½	11½	12½
	Continentale	㉚	38	39	41	42	43	44	46
Men's coats, jackets and suits	Britannica	34	36	38	40	42	44		
	Americana	34	36	38	40	42	44		
	Continentale	44	46	48	50	52	54		
Men's shirts	Britannica	14	14½	15	15½	16	16½	17	17½
	Americana	14	14½	15	15½	16	16½	17	17½
	Continentale	36	37	38	39	40	41	42	43

You   Vorrei un _____ _____ _____ da tennis.

Commesso   Che numero ha?

You   _____. Quanto _____?

Commesso   Cinquantasei euro.

You   Mi fa uno _____?

Commesso   Mi dispiace ma abbiamo i prezzi fissi.

? Test yourself

With the help of the words in the box, fill in the spaces.

quant'	scatoletta	pacchetto/confezione
dozzina	scatoletta	piccante
bottiglia	fresco	sacchetto

a una _____ di tonno

b una _____ di caffè macinato

c un etto di formaggio non troppo _____

d una _____ di pomodori pelati

e una _____ di olio di oliva

f una _____ di uova

g È _____ questo pesce?

h un _____ di piselli surgelati

i Può mettere tutto in un _____?

j _____ è?

SELF CHECK

I CAN. . .

●	. . . ask the price of things
●	. . . buy food and clothes
●	. . . ask for a discount
●	. . . use numbers
●	. . . state quantities

12 Tocca a me!
It's my turn!

In this unit, you will:
- ▸ *learn about making public telephone calls in Italy.*
- ▸ *practise 'at the post office'.*
- ▸ *practise how to respond to queue-jumping.*
- ▸ *learn how to change money at the bank.*
- ▸ *learn some Internet vocabulary.*
- ▸ *revise numbers (Units 3, 4, 5).*
- ▸ *revise how to ask for something (Unit 5).*

CEFR: (A2) *Can understand simple instructions on equipment encountered in everyday life – such as a public telephone.*

Read out loud the passage about changing money in Italy and answer the questions below.

Cambiare la valuta in Italia
Changing money in Italy

Per cambiare la valuta in Italia si può andare in banca o all'ufficio cambi ma il modo più pratico è quello di usare il cambiavalute elettronico che si trova negli aeroporti e, in grandi città, nelle stazioni e nelle banche. Generalmente fuori dalle banche c'è il bancomat cash dispenser dove si possono prelevare euro con la carta di credito. Le banche aprono dal lunedì al venerdì dalle 8.30 a.m. alle 1.20 p.m.. Generalmente aprono anche il pomeriggio, tra le 3 p.m. e le 4 p.m.. Il sabato, la domenica e durante i giorni festivi sono chiuse. Le banconote sono da 5, 10, 20, 50, 100, 200 e 500 euro. Le monete sono da 1, 2, 5, 10, 20 e 50 centesimi e da 1 e 2 euro.

1 **Dove si trovano i cambiavalute automatici?**

2 **Generalmente quando sono aperte le banche il pomeriggio?**

3 **Il sabato sono aperte?**

4 **Qual è la banconota di taglio più grande?**

5 **E la moneta euro più piccola?**

> **TIP**
> As you may have noticed from the passage, **euro** doesn't change in the plural in Italian.

Comunicazione e denaro
Communications and money

12.01

telefono	*telephone*
Devo telefonare…	*I must telephone…*
Devo fare una telefonata.	*I must make a telephone call.*
Devo guardare sull'elenco/guida telefonico/sulla guida telefonica.	*I must look in the telephone directory.*
carta/scheda telefonica	*phonecard*
comporre/fare il numero	*dial the number*
urbana	*local (call)*
interurbana	*trunk/long-distance (call)*
Qual è il prefisso?	*What's the code?*
Deve chiamare l'operatore.	*You must call the operator.*
una cabina telefonica	*a telephone booth*
Si è interrotta la linea.	*The line was cut off.*
È occupato.	*It's engaged.*
Richiamo.	*I'll call again.*
La linea è libera ma non risponde nessuno.	*The line is free but there is no answer.*
insegna/simbolo	*sign/symbol*
indicare	*to show*
funzionare	*to work, function*
chiedere/richiedere	*to ask for, require*
telefonata a carico del destinatario	*reverse-charge call/call collect*
la segreteria telefonica	*answering machine*
la segreteria telefonica centralizzata	*call minder*
il cellulare/il telefonino	*mobile/cellular phone*
posta	*post office/mail*

un francobollo per…	a stamp for…
spedire/inviare/mandare	to send
una cartolina	a card
posta prioritaria	first class (letter/parcel)
una busta	an envelope
il codice di avviamento postale	post/zip code
l'indirizzo	address
il mittente	the sender's address
lo sportello	window/counter
Ho fatto mezz'ora di coda.	I have been queueing/lining up for half an hour.
Posso passare avanti?	Can I go in front of you?
Ho molta fretta.	I am in a real hurry.
la buca delle lettere	letter/mail box
ufficio cambi	exchange bureau
firmi qui	sign here
il denaro/i soldi	money
valuta estera	foreign currency
contante	cash
cambiare sterline in euro	to exchange pounds into euros
dollari/assegno turistico	dollars/traveller's cheques
incassare un assegno	to cash a cheque
Quant' è il cambio?	What is the rate of exchange?
S'accomodi alla cassa.	Please go to the cash window/desk.
biglietto/banconota	banknote
grosso taglio	large denomination
spiccioli/monete	small change/small coins
il tasso (di cambio)/il cambio	rate (of exchange)
il bancomat	cash dispenser
la posta elettronica	email
www (read vu vu vu)	worldwide web
punto (.)	dot
barra (/)	slash
chiocciola (@)	'at' sign (@)
il sito	site
la rete/il web	net, web
cliccare	to click
informatica	computer science

l'internet	Internet
il fax	fax (machine)

DIALOGO 1

 12.02 Marcella desidera fare una telefonata a Londra e va all'ufficio turistico. Qual è il prefisso per l'Inghilterra?

Marcella	Vorrei telefonare in Inghilterra.
Impiegata	Si accomodi alla cabina cinque.
Marcella	Qual è il prefisso?
Impiegata	0044.
(After a while, Marcella emerges from the phone booth.)	
Marcella	Prima si è interrotta la linea. Adesso è occupato. Richiamo più tardi.
(later)	Adesso la linea è libera ma non risponde nessuno.

 ## PRATICA 1

You go to the tourist office to make a telephone call.

You	*Say that you want to make a telephone call.*
Impiegata	Si accomodi alla cabina uno.
You	*Say that you haven't the number.*
Impiegata	Che città desidera chiamare?
You	*Rome.*
Impiegata	Ha l'indirizzo?
You	*After giving the address, you ask what the code is.*
Impiegata	Il prefisso è 06 e il numero che mi ha richiesto è 123456.
You	*Say that the line is engaged. You will call later.*

PRATICA 2

Complete the following:

Lei è a Genova e desidera fare una _____ ad un amico che abita a Roma ma non sa il _____ di telefono. Deve guardare sull' _____ _____. È una telefonata _____: prima deve fare il _____ e poi il _____. Non risponde nessuno: è _____!

DIALOGO 2

Mr Simpson deve spedire una lettera e un pacco ma ha una difficoltà.

Mr Simpson	Vorrei spedire questa lettera e questo pacco.
Impiegata	Per il pacco deve andare all'altro sportello.
Mr Simpson	Ma io ho fatto mezz'ora di coda!
Impiegata	A questo sportello non si accettano pacchi.
(Mr Simpson joins another queue/line.)	
Signora	Scusi, posso passare avanti? Sa, ho molta fretta…
Mr Simpson	Mi dispiace ma anch'io ho molta fretta!

PRATICA 3

You are at the post office.

  a Say that you are sorry, but it's your turn.
  b Say that you wish to send an express letter to Scotland.
  c Ask the clerk if he has an envelope.
  d Ask if the stamp for a card costs as much as (**quanto**) a stamp for a letter.
  e Ask how much is the stamp for a card to the United States.

DIALOGO 3

 12.03 **Mrs Perkins va in banca a cambiare delle sterline in euro: quant'è il cambio oggi?**

Mrs Perkins	Vorrei cambiare cento sterline in euro.
Impiegato	Mi può dare il passaporto?
Mrs Perkins	Eccolo. Quant'è il cambio oggi?
Impiegato	Uno e cinquanta. Qual è il suo indirizzo in Italia?
Mrs Perkins	Albergo San Giorgio, Santa Margherita.
Impiegato	Firmi qui, per favore. Grazie. S'accomodi alla cassa.
(at the cash desk)	
Cassiere	Come vuole la valuta?
Mrs Perkins	Mi dia biglietti di grosso taglio e cinque euro in spiccioli.

You go to the bank to change some dollars and some traveller's cheques.

You	*Say that you would like to change $200 into euros.*
Impiegato	Ha il passaporto?
You	*Say yes, here it is.*
Impiegato	Qual è il suo indirizzo in Italia?
You	*Hotel Pitosforo. Say that you would also like to change a traveller's cheque.*
Impiegato	L'assegno è in euro?
You	*Say yes and ask what the rate of exchange is today.*
Impiegato	Uno e dieci. S'accomodi alla cassa.
(at the cash desk)	
Cassiera	Firmi qui, per favore. Ecco 160 euro.
You	*You would like large denomination notes and five euros in coins. Thank her and say goodbye.*

PRATICA 5

You are walking along the street and, as you see each of the signs below, you remember that you need (or must do) something. Choose two of the sentences, as appropriate, for each sign.

1

2

3

1 _____ and _____.

2 _____ and _____.

3 _____ and _____.

CELLULARI *MOBILE PHONES*

12.04 Here are some useful expressions relating to mobile phones.

cellulare (m.)/telefonino	*mobile phone*
numero di cellulare	*mobile phone number*
La batteria è scarica.	*The battery's run out.*
Devo ricaricare la batteria.	*I must charge the battery.*
Non trovo/Ho dimenticato il caricatore/il caricabatteria.	*I can't find/I forgot the charger.*
caricatore da auto	*car charger*
navigatore (m.) satellitare	*SATNAV*
auricolare (m.)	*hands-free headset*
vivavoce (m.)	*hands-free car kit*
adattatore (m.)	*adaptor*
Non c'è campo.	*There is no signal.* (lit. *There is no field.*)
Ho inviato/ricevuto un messaggino/un SMS (*pronounced* esse emme esse).	*I have sent/received a text.*
la ricarica	*top-up (money)*
la SIM card/la carta SIM	*SIM card*

ASCOLTA E SCRIVI *LISTEN AND WRITE*

12.05 **Listen to the dictation and write down what you hear. Then check your spelling against the passage at the beginning of this unit.**

? Test yourself

1 **Ask for the following items or information.**
   a 12 stamps for Great Britain
   b what the postcode for Rome is
   c if the sender's address is necessary
   d if they have a directory
   e what the rate of exchange is today
   f where the mail box is
   g whether the cheque is in dollars or pounds

2 **How do you say the following?**
   a I wish to send this letter first class.
   b I would like to change these Australian dollars into euros.
   c I must make a telephone call.
   d I must buy a new charger for (**per**) my mobile phone.
   e Is there a socket near the table?

SELF CHECK

I CAN. . .
● . . . make a telephone call
● . . . ask about opening times
● . . . say what I want to do
● . . . change money

In giro per la città
Going about town

In this unit, you will:

▶ *learn how to ask for, understand and give simple street directions.*

▶ *learn how to understand information about public transport.*

▶ *revise how to ask where something is (Unit 3).*

▶ *revise how to ask for information and tickets (Unit 7).*

▶ *revise how to say what you want to do (Unit 8).*

▶ *revise how to talk about the things you do (Unit 9).*

CEFR: (A2) *Can understand and give simple directions relating to how to get from X to Y, by foot or on public transport.*

I trasporti pubblici *Public transport*

In tutte le città e nei luoghi di villeggiatura (*holiday resorts*) si possono trovare tassì vicino alla stazione e nelle parti principali della città. Naturalmente i tassì si possono anche chiamare per telefono. Normalmente non si possono fermare per la strada/in marcia. Le tariffe variano da posto a posto e generalmente durante la notte sono più care. Viaggiare in autobus è piuttosto economico. Nelle città la maggior parte degli autobus non ha il bigliettaio (*bus conductor*) ma una macchina che timbra (*stamps*) il biglietto con la data e l'ora: quindi è necessario comprare il biglietto prima di salire sull'autobus! I biglietti si comprano all'ufficio turistico, in edicola, in tabaccheria e in alcuni bar. Su alcuni autobus è possibile comprare il biglietto dall'autista (*driver*) ma a un prezzo maggiorato (*higher price*). In alcuni luoghi, alla stazione dell'autobus ci sono distributori automatici (*vending machines*) di biglietti.

HA CAPITO? *HAVE YOU UNDERSTOOD?*

1 Il prezzo dei biglietti per l'autobus è alto?

2 Dove si comprano i biglietti per l'autobus?

3 Costa meno comprare i biglietti sull'autobus?

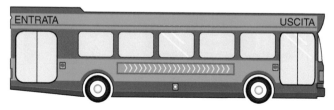

Come andare a... *How to get to...*

13.01

fermata	*bus stop*
trovare	*to find*
Va avanti dritto.	*You go straight ahead.*
principale ♣	*main*
Gira a destra/a sinistra.	*You turn right/left.*
prende…	*take…*
la prima a destra	*the first on the right*
la seconda a sinistra	*the second on the left*
alla fine della strada	*at the end of the road*
all'altro lato della piazza	*at the other end of the square*
di fronte al duomo	*opposite the cathedral*
dietro la stazione	*behind the station*
sotto la torre dell'orologio	*under the clock tower*
dopo il semaforo	*after the traffic lights*
Attraversa il ponte.	*You cross the bridge.*
i giardini	*gardens*
chiedere/domandare	*to ask*
andare a piedi	*to go on foot*
Mi sono perso/a.	*I am lost.*
Deve tornare indietro.	*You must go back.*
porto	*harbour/port*
il pontile (d'imbarco)/l'imbarcadero	*jetty/landing stage*
lungomare	*sea-front/promenade*
battello	*boat*
vaporetto	*water bus*
Che cosa significa…?	*What does… mean?*

UN BIGLIETTO *A TICKET*

1 Answer these questions about the bus ticket.

LATO DI CONVALIDA	GR 11 – SERIE T
cpt Compania Pisana Transporti s.p.a.	**N.0106424**
	BIGLIETTO ORARIO **€ 0,80**
VALE 60 MINUTI RETE URBANA	Cassa di risparmio di volterra s.p.A. 27 Filiali nella provincia

a Per quanto tempo può viaggiare in città con questo biglietto?

b Quanto costa il biglietto?

c Bisogna convalidare il biglietto?

DIALOGO 1

 13.02 **Un turista chiede informazioni ad un passante (*passer-by*).**

Turista	Scusi, sa dov'è la fermata dell'autobus?
Passante	Dove deve andare?
Turista	In piazza Acquaverde.
Passante	La fermata è alla fine di questa strada a sinistra, vicino al supermercato.
Turista	Vicino al supermercato, a destra.
Passante	No, a sinistra.
Turista	È lontano?
Passante	Cinque minuti da qui.
Turista	Sa che autobus devo prendere?
Passante	Il numero 27.
Turista	Molte grazie.

 PRATICA 1

13.03 **Complete this dialogue between you and a passer-by.**

You	Scusi, dov'è la _____ dell'autobus?
Passante	È all' _____ _____ della piazza.
You	L'autobus per la stazione ferma a destra o a _____?
Passante	A destra.
You	La stazione è _____?

PRATICA 2

Imagine you are trying to find your way in an Italian city. You stop a passer-by and ask where the fish market (il mercato del pesce) is.

> **TIP**
> When in Italy, if you don't understand what is said to you, do not hesitate to ask: **Può/Puoi ripetere, per favore?** *Could you repeat that, please?* **Può/Puoi parlare lentamente?** *Could you speak more slowly?* **Come ha/hai detto?** *What did you say?* is also commonly used.

You	*Ask where the fish market is.*
Passante	Il mercato del pesce? È in piazza Matteotti.
You	*Ask where piazza Matteotti is.*
Passante	È la prima strada a sinistra.
You	*Ask if it is far.*
Passante	No, due minuti.
You	*Ask if there is a bookshop in piazza Matteotti.*
Passante	No, ce n'è una in via Dante. Sa dov'è?
You	*Say no, can you go on foot?*
Passante	No, è troppo lontano. Deve prendere l'autobus.
You	*Ask where the bus stop is.*
Passante	È alla fine della strada. Vicino al semaforo.
You	*Thank him very much and say goodbye.*

PRATICA 3

You are asked where the fish market is. You have just been there; give directions, using the map below.

Va _____ _____, poi prende la _____ _____ _____.

Il mercato è all' _____ _____ _____ piazza, vicino ai _____.

DIALOGO 2

 13.04 **Un gruppo di turisti des_i_dera andare da Santa Margherita a Portofino in battello.**

Turista	Scusi, da dove p_a_rtono i battelli per Portofino?
Passante	Deve andare sul lungomare.
Turista	È lontano da qui?
Passante	No, va avanti dritto e quando arriva alla piazza con i giardini vede il pontile d'imbarco per i battelli: è prima del porto.
Turista	Molte grazie.
Passante	Prego.

PRATICA 4

 13.05 **After a few days in Venice, you have become an expert at finding your way around. An Italian tourist stops you and asks you the way to Piazza San Marco.**

Turista	Scusi, sa dov'è Piazza San Marco?
You	*You must cross the bridge.*
Turista	Attraverso il ponte e poi?
You	*Then you take the first on the left and go straight on. At the end of the road, you'll see Piazza San Marco.*

ASCOLTA E SCRIVI *LISTEN AND WRITE*

 TIP

 13.06 **Listen to the dictation and write down what you hear. Then check your spelling against the passage at the beginning of this unit.**

After doing each dictation, it is advisable to listen to it once more, checking the spelling yourself, before checking it against the passage.

⑦ Test yourself

Do you remember how to say the following?

a I'm lost.
b opposite the cathedral
c You must go back.
d before the harbour
e after the traffic lights
f behind the station
g opposite the baker's
h under the clock tower
i near the gardens
j Can I go on foot?

SELF CHECK

I CAN. . .
⚫ . . . understand and give simple directions
⚫ . . . ask for information
⚫ . . . understand information about public transport
⚫ . . . buy tickets

14 Un alloggio
Accommodation

In this unit, you will:

▶ *practise finding accommodation, checking in and paying the bill.*

▶ *learn how to deal with some problems at hotels and campsites.*

▶ *practise spelling out your name.*

▶ *revise how to ask for something (Unit 5).*

▶ *revise how to talk about things that have happened (Unit 10).*

▶ *revise how to ask the price of something (Unit 5).*

▶ *revise expressions of time (Unit 6).*

CEFR: (A2) *Can deal with common aspects of everyday living such as travel and lodgings.*

 ## Un posto per dormire *A place to stay*

Ci sono circa 40.000 alberghi in Italia e sono classificati in categorie: cinque stelle de lux (***** de lux), cinque stelle (*****), quattro stelle (****), tre stelle (***), due stelle (**) e una stella (*). I *bed and breakfast* sono camere in case private, ufficialmente riconosciute (*officially recognized*). Nei motel (o alberghi meublè) non c'è ristorante ma spesso servono la prima colazione (*breakfast*). L'agriturismo (*farm holidays*) offre ospitalità in zone rurali dove si può vivere in armonia con la natura in zone tranquille e a prezzi convenienti. Ci sono in Italia anche molti conventi e monasteri in zone tranquille che offrono vitto e alloggio (*board and lodging*) a prezzi modici (*reasonable*). Gli ostelli per la gioventù (*youth hostels*) e le case dello studente sono reservati a giovani (*young people*) e a studenti e hanno prezzi bassi. In tutta Italia c'è anche una grande varietà di campeggi (chiamati anche *camping*). I prezzi degli alberghi includono le tasse ma normalmente la prima colazione non è inclusa nel prezzo eccetto quando si è a pensione completa o a mezza pensione. La patente italiana può essere accettata come documento d'identità.

1 **Sono più cari gli alberghi o gli ostelli?**

2 **Una persona anziana può andare in un ostello per la gioventù?**

3 **Con la mezza pensione si deve pagare separatamente la prima colazione?**

4 **Si può cenare (*to dine*) in un meublè?**

5 **Nei conventi e nei monasteri i prezzi sono alti?**

IN ALBERGO *AT THE HOTEL*

14.01

cercare	*to look for*
Ha/Avete…	*Have you got…*
una camera libera?	*a free/vacant room?*
singola/doppia	*single/double*
matrimoniale/a due letti	*with a double bed/with twin beds*
con/senza bagno	*with/without a bath*
con/senza doccia	*with/without a shower*
pensione completa/mezza pensione	*full board/half board*
Mi dà…?	*May I have…? (lit. Will you give me…?)*
la carta d'identità	*identity card*
la patente	*driving licence*
la chiave	*key*
il facchino	*porter*
la valigia	*suitcase*
la carta di credito	*credit card*
gli assegni turistici	*traveller's cheques*
gli assegni (bancari)	*(personal) cheques*
C'è un errore/uno sbaglio nel conto.	*There is a mistake in the bill/check.*
Mi scusi tanto.	*I do apologize, I'm very sorry.*
accettare	*to accept*
lasciare	*to leave*
la portineria/la reception	*reception/front desk*
subito	*at once*
in anticipo	*beforehand*
la sera prima	*the evening before*
Desidero la sveglia alle…	*I would like a wake-up call at…*

DIALOGO 1

Una turista chiede (*asks for*) informazioni all'ufficio turistico sugli alberghi della città. Che tipo di albergo desidera?

Turista	Buongiorno. Mio marito ed io cerchiamo una camera per questa notte.
Impiegata	Questa è la lista degli alberghi della città.
Turista	Ci può consigliare un albergo tranquillo e non troppo caro?
Impiegata	L'albergo San Giorgio e il Piccolo Hotel sono molto tranquilli. Se vuole telefono per vedere se ci sono camere libere.
Turista	Sì, grazie.

PRATICA 1

 Ask if the hotel has the following facilities.

a L'albergo è in una ●◀ ?

b C'è il 🌲 ?

c C'è l' ⬆⬇ nell'albergo?

d C'è l' 🚗 ?

e C'è la 🌊 ?

f L'albergo è in una ⊗ ?

g Nelle camere c'è l' ▭ ?

h C'è il ☎ ?

i C'è anche il TV ?

j E il 🔥 c'è?

You are at the tourist office looking for a suitable hotel.

You	*Say good morning, you are looking for a hotel in a quiet position.*
Impiegata	L'albergo Giardini e il Piccolo Parco sono molto tranquilli.
You	*Ask which is the best.*
Impiegata	Ma… dipende un po' dalle sue preferenze… il Piccolo Parco è più tranquillo ma il Giardini è in una posizione panoramica.
You	*Say that Piccolo Parco is OK and ask if she can phone and see if there are any rooms available.*
Impiegata	Che tipo di camera vuole?
You	*You want a single room with shower.*

DIALOGO 2

14.02 **Sergio e Francesca desiderano una camera per tre notti.**

Portiere	Buonasera, signori.
Sergio	Buonasera. Ha una camera libera?
Portiere	Singola o doppia?
Sergio	Doppia.
Portiere	Matrimoniale o a due letti?
Sergio	A due letti, con bagno.
Portiere	Mi dispiace, ma non abbiamo camere libere con bagno: soltanto con doccia.
Francesca	Con doccia va bene. Quanto costa la camera?
Portiere	Centoventi euro per notte.
Sergio	Va bene, la prendiamo.
Portiere	Per quante notti?
Sergio	Per tre notti.
Portiere	Camera 225 al secondo piano. Ecco la chiave. Mi dà i documenti, per favore?
Sergio	Ecco la carta d'identità.
Francesca	Va bene la patente?
Portiere	Certamente, signora. Grazie.

PRATICA 3

Give the questions in Italian for these answers.

a Per tre notti.

b La camera costa centoventi euro per notte.

c Sì, la patente va benissimo.

You could now play with Dialogue 2 by changing as much as you can of what is said by Sergio, Francesca and the concierge/porter (e.g. **per una settimana**; **due camere singole**, etc.).

DIALOGO 3

Sergio e Francesca pagano il conto e trovano un errore.

Portiere	Buongiorno, signori.
Sergio	Il conto, per favore.
Portiere	Ecco il conto, signore.
Sergio	Che cos'è questo?
Portiere	La prima colazione, signore.
Francesca	Ma noi non abbiamo fatto colazione: c'è un errore!
Portiere	Ha ragione, signora; mi scusi tanto.
Sergio	Posso pagare con la carta di credito?
Portiere	Certamente signore, accettiamo carta di credito, valuta estera, assegni… tutto.
Sergio	A che ora dobbiamo lasciare la camera?
Portiere	A mezzogiorno. Se vuole può lasciare le valigie in portineria.
Sergio	Non è necessario. Il facchino le può portare in macchina?
Portiere	Certamente, lo chiamo subito.

PRATICA 4

Read Dialogue 3 and then fill in the gaps.

a Sergio chiede _____ _____ al portiere.

b Sergio e Francesca non _____ _____ colazione.

c C'è _____ _____ nel conto.

PRATICA 5

Imagine you are staying in a hotel. There is quite a lot wrong with your room. Use the expressions Vorrei un altro (un'altra)…, Non funziona… or Non c'è… as appropriate in relation to the following.

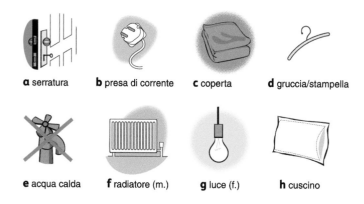

a serratura   **b** presa di corrente   **c** coperta   **d** gruccia/stampella

e acqua calda   **f** radiatore (m.)   **g** luce (f.)   **h** cuscino

IN CAMPEGGIO *AT THE CAMPSITE*

14.03

prenotare/riservare	*to book/reserve*
prenotazione	*reservation*
tenda	*tent*
parcheggiare la roulotte/il camper	*to park the caravan/camper/trailer*
Che servizi ci sono?	*What facilities are there?*
Dov'è l'acqua potabile?	*Where is the drinking water?*
la bombola del gas	*gas bottle*
la presa di corrente	*electric socket*
forse	*perhaps, maybe*
cartello	*sign*
nome (*m.*)	*name, first name*
cognome (*m.*)	*surname*
Come si scrive?	*How do you spell it?*

DIALOGO 4

 14.04 **Before listening to Dialogue 4, play track 14.04 and follow the exercise in Pratica 7. This will help you with the Italian alphabet.**

14.05 **Il signore e la signora Hazeltine arrivano in un campeggio senza prenotazione.**

Signor H.	Avete il posto per un camper?
Impiegata	Per quante notti?
Signor H.	Cinque notti. Forse di più.
Impiegata	Ho un posto per cinque notti soltanto.
Signor H.	Va bene.
Impiegata	Il suo nome per favore?
Signor H.	Hazeltine.
Impiegata	Come si scrive?
Signor H.	Acca, a, zeta, e, elle, ti, i, enne, e. Dov'è il posto per il camper?
Impiegata	Va avanti dritto, poi gira a destra e vede il cartello 'CAMPERS'.
Signor H.	Che servizi ci sono?
Impiegata	Bagni, docce, gabinetti, un negozio…
Signor H.	La presa della corrente c'è?
Impiegata	Certamente. Se ha bisogno di una bombola di gas la può richiedere al negozio.

PRATICA 6

Answer these questions:

a Which of the two campsites shown below could you use in winter?

b What discount would you get at the Frassanito campsite if you were a member of Federcampeggio?

c Would you go to the Frassanito if you wanted a holiday in the countryside?

VILLAGGIO TURISTICO SPORTIVO
SAN GIORGIO
CAMPEGGIO INTERNAZIONALE
70040 BARI - S.S. 16 al km. 809 deviazone per
S. Giorigio km. 6 a sud di Bari
Tel. 491175-491202-491226

Aperto tutto l'anno – Bungalows – Alloggi – Trulli –
Complesso nautico con rimessaggio e assistenza – Articoli
de campeggio e turismo – Assistenza Caravan – Bar –
Tabacchi – Alimentari – Macelleria – Spaccio frutta e
verdura – Market – Pizzeria – Tavola calda – Pattinaggio
Hockey – Tennis – Bocce – Palestra – Sala Attrazioni-
Complesso balneare con piscina e parco gionchi per
bambini – Ufficio Postale – Chiesa

```
OTRANTO (Lecce)    aperto da
"Frassanito"       aprile a
– A 12km. a        settembre
nord-ovest di      sconti. 10%
Otranto – Sul      AIT-FIA-FICC
mare – Tel         20%
(0836) 85005       Federcampeggio
```

PRATICA 7

14.04 **Read the alphabet out loud and practise spelling out your nome, cognome and indirizzo.**

			L'alfabeto	*The alphabet*		
A	B	C	D	E	F	G
a	bi	ci	di	e	effe	gi
H	I	J	K	L	M	N
acca	i	i-lunga/jay	cappa	elle	emme	enne
O	P	Q	R	S	T	U
o	pi	cu	erre	esse	ti	u
V	W	X	Y	Z		
vu	doppio-vu	ics	ipsilon	zeta		

Now practise by spelling out names of your choice: family, friends, pets, food... what about *Worcestershire sauce*?

PRATICA 8

 Read the following passage.

Soggiorno in albergo *Staying in a hotel*

> Quando va in vacanza deve prenotare l'albergo
> in anticipo. Deve dire se desidera una camera con
> bagno o senza bagno; se vuole soltanto la camera,
> se preferisce stare a mezza pensione o a pensione
> completa. Se prende soltanto la camera chiede se la
> prima colazione è compresa (inclusa) nel prezzo.
> Vuole anche sapere se l'albergo accetta la carta di
> credito o altri tipi di pagamento come gli assegni
> turistici. Quando arriva chiede anche: dove **posso**
> **parcheggiare? Può far portare i bagagli in**
> **camera? A che ora è la prima colazione? A che**
> **ora è il pranzo? A che ora è la cena?** Se al mattino
> deve alzarsi presto la sera prima dice: **domani**
> **mattina desidero la sveglia alle**… Se qualcosa
> non funziona o la camera non è tranquilla informa
> subito il direttore.

 Now say the sentences below in Italian.
   a Tell reception that you wish to be called at six tomorrow.
   b Ask where you can park.
   c Ask reception for a porter to take your case to your room.

 In the above passage, there are 15 verbs in the present tense, third person singular (the formal *you*). Can you change them into the first person singular (io)? Quando vado in vacanza devo…. As you know, andare and volere are irregular verbs and alzarsi is a reflexive verb in the infinitive form (Unit 9).

ASCOLTA E SCRIVI LISTEN AND WRITE

 14.07 **Listen to the dictation and write down what you hear. Then check your spelling in the Key.**

? Test yourself

Try to say the following in Italian.

a This is room 209.

b There is no hot water in the bathroom.

c The shower doesn't work.

d Have you got a list of the hotels for this town?

e Have you got a place for a caravan?

f Where is the drinking water?

g Have you got a double room with a bathroom?

h Where is the electric socket?

i How do you spell your surname?

j Can you give me your passport/documents?

SELF CHECK

I CAN. . .
. . . check in and out of hotels
. . . spell my name
. . . talk about things that have happened
. . . deal with difficulties at hotels and campsites

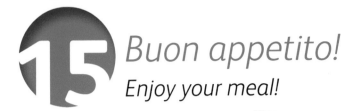

15 Buon appetito!
Enjoy your meal!

In this unit, you will:
▸ *learn about Italian meals.*
▸ *practise how to ask for the table you prefer.*
▸ *learn how to find out if you will like a particular dish.*
▸ *learn how to order drinks and meals.*
▸ *revise how to express likes and dislikes (Unit 4).*
▸ *revise how to ask for something (Unit 5).*
▸ *revise how to say what you want to do (Unit 8).*

CEFR: (A2) *Can read and understand menus, and order a meal.*

 ## Mangiare bene *Eating well*

 15.01 Gli italiani hanno una particolare attenzione per i cibi freschi e genuini (*wholesome*). La cucina italiana vanta (*boasts*) una grande quantità di specialità culinarie che variano da regione a regione.

Oltre che (*Besides/As well as*) al **ristorante**, si può mangiare bene anche in **pizzeria** o in **rosticceria**. Se non si ha un enorme appetito si può andare a una **tavola calda**, in **paninoteca** (un negozio specializzato in panini imbottiti) o in un **bar** dove, oltre a dolci e gelati, si possono prendere panini imbottiti, tramezzini, toast (pronuncia **tòst**); il toast è un *toasted sandwich*. Oggi alcuni bar offrono anche un pasto caldo. Per chi viaggia in automobile in autostrada ci sono gli **autogrill** che offrono panini e cibi pronti. Se si desidera qualcosa di più sostanzioso ci sono **ristoranti**, **trattorie**, e **osterie**. La trattoria è spesso gestita da una famiglia, il cibo è casalingo e i prezzi sono moderati. Anche nelle osterie si mangiano cibi casalinghi, spesso specialità locali.

15.02

1 Che cosa vende la paninoteca?
2 Che cosa bisogna dire in un bar per avere un **toasted sandwich**?
3 Dove sono gli autogrill?
4 Che tipo di cibo si serve in una trattoria?

In the above passage, there are six impersonal expressions (*one can, if one*, etc.): si può mangiare; se non si ha; si può andare; si possono prendere; se si desidera; si mangiano. Can you read the passage again out loud, replacing the impersonal forms with the following tu forms?

puoi mangiare	se non hai	puoi andare
puoi prendere	se desideri	mangi

Mangiare fuori *Eating out*

15.03

tutto occupato	*all taken*
porta/finestra	*door/window*
tavola calda	*snack bar*
imbottito	*filled*
tramezzino	*sandwich*
autostrada	*motorway/highway*
abbastanza	*reasonably/fairly*
sostanzioso	*substantial*
gestire	*to run, manage*
a turno	*in turn, in rota*
saltare	*to skip* (lit. *to jump*), *to omit*
ordinare un pasto	*to order a meal*
pranzare	*to (have) lunch*
fare uno spuntino/una merenda	*to have a snack*
il piatto del giorno	*dish of the day*
il menú	*menu*
al forno/alla griglia	*cooked in the oven/grilled*
arrosto/bollito	*roasted/boiled*
saltato/brasato	*sautéd, lightly fried/braised*

fritto/impanata	*fried/breaded*
olio/aceto	*oil/vinegar*
sottaceti	*mixed pickles*
sale (m.)/pepe (m.)	*salt/pepper*
assortimento	*selection*
Prendo una bistecca.	*I'll have a steak.*
ben cotta/media/al sangue	*well done/medium/rare*
fatto in casa	*home-made*
bere	*to drink*
Che cosa beve/prende?	*What will you drink/have?*
Prendo un analcolico.	*I'll have a non-alcoholic aperitif.*
succo di frutta	*fruit juice*
spremuta d'arancia	*freshly squeezed orange juice*
acqua minerale gassata	*sparkling mineral water*
acqua minerale naturale/non gassata	*still mineral water*
digestivo	*digestive (liqueur)*
con/senza ghiaccio	*with/without ice*
secco/dolce	*dry/sweet*
Che cosa vuol dire…?	*What does… mean?*
Che cosa significa…?	*What does… mean?*
Come si dice…?	*How do you say…?*
mancia	*tip*
della casa	*of the house*
offre la casa	*it's on the house*

DIALOGO 1

Chiara e Roberto vanno in una trattoria con Paul e Anne.

Roberto	Buongiorno, ha un tavolo per quattro?
Cameriere	Hanno riservato?
Roberto	No. È possibile sedersi fuori?
Cameriere	Mi dispiace ma fuori è tutto occupato. Va bene qui?
Chiara	Questo tavolo è troppo vicino alla porta.
Cameriere	Vicino alla finestra va bene?
Chiara	Sì, grazie.
Cameriere	Desiderano un aperitivo?
Paul	Sì, grazie. Io prendo un Martini con ghiaccio.
Anne	Per me un succo di albicocca.
Chiara	Per me una spremuta d'arancia.
Roberto	Io prendo un analcolico.

PRATICA 1

You and your friend arrive at the same restaurant; this time there is a table available outside.

You	*Ask for a table for two.*
Cameriere	S'accomodino.
You	*Ask if you (both) can sit outside.*
Cameriere	Sì, c'è un tavolo libero. Desiderano un aperitivo?
You	*Order an alcohol-free aperitif and a tomato juice without ice.*

PRATICA 2

Read the following passage and answer the questions.

Piatti italiani *Italian dishes*

Il fritto misto può essere di carne o di pesce. Generalmente nelle località di mare consiste in calamari (*squid*) e piccoli pesci fritti. Nelle località lontano dal mare il fritto misto consiste in carni varie e verdure miste fritte. La *mustard* inglese in italiano si chiama **senape**. La **zuppa inglese** non è una zuppa ma è un dolce simile al *trifle* inglese, con liquore (rum e alkermes), crema pasticceria e cioccolato. **Alla casalinga** significa fatto in casa. In quasi tutti i ristoranti c'è un menù a prezzo fisso e una lista dei piatti del giorno. Un pasto completo consiste in antipasto (prosciutto e melone, salame, eccetera), il primo piatto (zuppa, minestrone o pasta), il secondo piatto (carne o pesce) con contorno (*side dish*) di verdure o insalata (*salad*) e il dolce (o formaggio e frutta).

   a Con quale piatto è servito il contorno?
   b Nelle località di campagna che cosa servono come fritto misto?
   c La zuppa inglese ha verdure?

MENÙ

Antipasti
antipasto misto
verdure ripiene
acciughe al limone
prosciutto e melone o fichi

Primi Piatti
zuppa di verdura
spaghetti ai funghi
risotto di mare
fettuccine alla panna

Secondi Piatti
scaloppine al marsala
bistecca alla griglia
cotoletta alla milanese
brasato con lenticchie
pollo alla cacciatora
fegato alla veneziana
pesce al cartoccio
agnello arrosto

Contorni
spinaci al burro o limone
piselli al prezzemolo
fagiolini al burro
patate al forno e bollite
insalata mista

Formaggi Assortiti

Frutta e Dolce
frutta di stagione
zuppa inglese
torta della casa
gelati assortiti

☆

Servizio incluso

☆

 Chiara e Roberto discutono *(discuss)* il menù con i loro amici australiani Paul e Anne.

Roberto	Cameriere, può portare il menù?
Cameriere	Subito, signori. Ecco il menù.
Paul	In che cosa consiste l'antipasto misto?
Roberto	L'antipasto misto è un assortimento di verdure ripiene, salame, prosciutto, sottaceti…
Anne	Che cos'è il risotto di mare?
Chiara	*Seafood* risotto, con frutti di mare.
Paul	**Panna** vuol dire *cream*, non è vero?
Chiara	Sì. So che qui il pesce al cartoccio è eccellente.
	È pesce al forno, come si dice… *in a paper case.*
Anne	E il fegato alla veneziana?
Roberto	Il fegato è *liver.* È fritto con cipolle e alloro (*bay leaf*).

PRATICA 3

Now it's your turn to ask.

You	*What is* **manzo brasato con lenticchie***?*
Cameriere	Braised beef with lentils.
You	*What does* **marsala** *mean?*
Cameriere	È un tipo di vino siciliano.
You	*Is* **cotoletta alla milanese** *fried meat?*
Cameriere	Sì: impanata e fritta.
You	*How do you say chop in Italian?*
Cameriere	Braciola.

DIALOGO 3

15.04 **Roberto, Chiara e i loro amici ordinano il pasto.**

Cameriere	Desiderano ordinare?
Roberto	Sì, grazie. *(to Anne)* Tu che cosa prendi Anne?
Anne	Io prendo un antipasto misto e scaloppine al Marsala. Salto il primo piatto.
Cameriere	E come contorno?
Anne	Spinaci al limone e patate al forno.
Chiara	E tu, Paul?
Paul	Per me acciughe *(anchovies)* al limone e una bistecca alla griglia. Come contorno piselli al prezzemolo e carciofi fritti.
Cameriere	Come vuole la bistecca?
Paul	Media.
Chiara	Io prendo prosciutto crudo con fichi e risotto di mare.
Roberto	Per me fettuccine alla panna e fegato alla veneziana. Per contorno patate bollite e fagiolini al burro.
Cameriere	Da bere che cosa prendono?
Robert	Una bottiglia di vino bianco secco e una caraffa di vino rosso della casa.
Anne	E una bottiglia di acqua minerale.

PRATICA 4

15.05 **Your friend doesn't speak Italian, so you order for both of you.**

Cameriere	Desiderano ordinare?
You	*Yes, thank him and say that you will skip the hors d'oeuvres and have vegetable soup and roast lamb.*
Cameriere	E come contorno?
You	*As a side dish, you will have fried artichokes and roast potatoes.*
Cameriere	E il signore?
You	*The gentleman will have stuffed vegetables and chicken cacciatora with salad.*
Cameriere	Da bere?
You	*Half a carafe of red house wine and half a bottle of mineral water.*

DIALOGO 4

Alla fine del pasto il cameriere ritorna con il menù.

Cameriere	Tutto bene?
Roberto	Sì, grazie.
Cameriere	Desiderano dolce, gelato, formaggio?
Chiara	Io vorrei un po' di frutta. Tu, Anne?
Anne	Anch'io preferisco frutta fresca.
Paul	Io prendo la zuppa inglese.
Roberto	Per me un gelato misto (*ice cream of mixed flavours*).
Cameriere	Dopo desiderano il caffè? Un digestivo?
Roberto	Quattro caffè e il conto per favore.

PRATICA 5

The waiter comes back with the menu.

Cameriere	Tutto bene?
You	*Say yes, thank you.*
Cameriere	Desiderano un dolce?
You	*You would like the home-made cake, and for the gentleman some cheese.*
Cameriere	Dopo desiderano un caffè? Un digestivo?
You	*A liqueur, a coffee and the bill, please.*

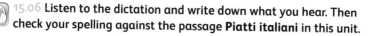

15.06 **Listen to the dictation and write down what you hear. Then check your spelling against the passage Piatti italiani in this unit.**

? Test yourself

How would you say the following to the waiter?

a There is too much salt in the soup.

b I would like some bread, please.

c The chicken is cold.

d The steak is not well done.

e There is no pepper on the table.

f What is the dish of the day?

g I'd like seafood spaghetti.

h I prefer still mineral water.

i Grilled fish, please.

j A bottle of white house wine, please

SELF CHECK

I CAN. . .
. . . understand a menu in Italian
. . . request a particular table in a restaurant
. . . find out if you will like a dish
. . . order drinks and a meal

16 Vita in famiglia
Family life

In this unit, you will:

▶ *practise talking about family and home.*
▶ *express how you feel and say if one is right or wrong.*
▶ *revise how to describe something (Unit 4).*
▶ *revise how to talk about the things you do (Unit 9).*
▶ *revise how to express preferences (Unit 4).*

CEFR: (A2) *Can use a series of phrases and sentences to describe family and living conditions in simple terms.*

 ## Case e appartamenti *Houses and flats*

 16.01 **Casa** significa *house* e *home*. Un edificio con appartamenti si chiama **palazzo** o **condominio**. Nei palazzi antichi, specialmente nel centro storico delle città, c'è ancora il portiere ma in quelli moderni, all'esterno, vicino all'ingresso principale, ci sono i campanelli di tutti i condomini e un citofono per comunicare con loro. Non tutte le persone posseggono l'appartamento in cui (*in which*) abitano: alcuni lo hanno in affitto. Affittare significa sia dare in affitto (*let*) che prendere in affitto (*rent*). Un appartamento con doppi servizi significa un appartamento con due bagni.

TIP
In certain cases, **casa** can also mean *building, block of flats* or *cottage*.

16.02 Vero o falso? *True or false?*

1 'Casa' può essere anche un appartamento.

2 Nei palazzi moderni c'è il portiere.

3 Tutti gli italiani hanno appartamenti in affitto.

4 Normalmente gli appartamenti hanno doppi servizi.

5 Affittare vuol dire 'dare' o 'prendere' in affitto.

Casa e giardino *House and garden*

16.03

il portiere (m.)	*doorman, janitor*
ingresso/campanello	*entrance/bell (push)*
condòmino/condomìnio	*co-owner/condominium*
compagno/compagna	*(live-in) partner*
ragazzo/ragazza	*boyfriend/girlfriend*
fidanzato/fidanzata	*fiancé/fiancée/steady boy or girlfriend*
citòfono	*intercom*
sia… che	*both… and*
dare/prendere in affitto	*to let/rent/lease*
fiori (di campo)	*(wild) flowers*
àlbero	*tree*
erbe aromàtiche	*herbs*
aglio	*garlic*
cucina	*kitchen*
studio	*study*
salotto	*living room*
sala da pranzo	*dining room*
caminetto	*fireplace*
mostrare	*to show*
portare	*to bring/carry*
aiutare a lavare i piatti	*to help do the washing-up/the dishes*
stirare	*to do the ironing*
spolverare	*to do the dusting*
rifare il letto	*to make the bed*

ANIMALI DOMESTICI *PETS*

il cane/la cagna	*dog/bitch*
il gatto/la gatta	*cat/female cat*
l'uccello	*bird*

EXPRESSING HOW YOU FEEL

essere	*to be*
felice/triste	*happy/sad*
stanco/a	*tired*
simpatico/a/antipatico/a	*pleasant/unpleasant*
preoccupato/a	*worried*
avere…	*to…*
caldo/freddo	*be hot/cold*
fame/sete	*be hungry/thirsty*
ragione/torto	*be right/wrong*
voglia di/bisogno di	*feel like/need*
d'accordo, allora	*that's settled, then*
con piacere	*with pleasure*
sono sicuro/a	*I'm sure*
ridere/scherzare	*to laugh/to joke*
contro	*against/versus*
una volta la settimana	*once a week*
Che bel giardino!	*What a beautiful garden!*
Chi lo cura?	*Who looks after it?*
il giardiniere	*gardener*
l'orto	*vegetable garden*
più che altro	*more than anything else*
Ho una passione per…	*I am very keen on…*
Ha proprio l'atmosfera	*It really has the atmosphere*
dei tempi passati	*of bygone times*

TIP

In the word list here, there are some expressions which are formed with *to be* in English but with **avere** *to have* in Italian:

- **Desidero bere perché ho sete.** *I want to drink because I'm thirsty.*
- **Vado a mangiare perché ho fame.** *I'm going to eat because I'm hungry.*
- **Chiudo la finestra perché ho freddo.** *I'm closing the window because I'm cold.*

156

16.04 Chiara ha invitato Francesca nella sua casa di campagna.

Francesca	Che bel giardino! Chi lo cura?
Chiara	Roberto ed io, quando siamo qui. Quando non ci siamo viene un giardiniere una volta la settimana. Più che altro noi curiamo l'orto. Io ho una passione per le erbe aromatiche: rosmarino, maggiorana, basilico… però mi piacciono anche i fiori di campo.
Francesca	Questo è aglio?
Chiara	Sì. Vieni, ti mostro la casa. Questa è la cucina: è un po' vecchia ma a noi piace.
Francesca	Ha proprio l'atmosfera dei tempi passati…
Chiara	Questo è il bagno, qui c'è il salotto… la sala da pranzo… al piano di sopra c'è la nostra camera e quella per gli ospiti, un piccolo studio e un altro bagno.
Francesca	Ah… vedo che avete il caminetto!
Chiara	Sì, qualche volta è un po' un problema. Vieni, andiamo in veranda.

Language discovery

Che can be used in exclamations:

▶ before a noun to express *What (a)…* !

Che peccato!	*What a pity!*
Che noia!	*What a nuisance!*

▶ before an adjective to translate *How…* !

Che bello!	*How nice!*
Che buffo!	*How funny!*

When **bello** *beautiful/nice/handsome* is followed by a noun, its ending imitates the definite article (**il**, **lo**, **la**, etc.).

bel fiore	*beautiful flower*
begli occhi	*beautiful eyes*
bell'idea	*nice idea*
bei ragazzi	*handsome boys*

> **TIP**
>
> Nowadays, **bagno** *bathroom* is also used instead of **gabinetto** or **toeletta** *toilet*:
> - **Devo andare in bagno.** *I must go to the toilet.*
> - **Mi scusi, dov' è il bagno?** *Excuse me, where is the toilet?*

PRATICA 1

Answer these questions by reshaping the question to form your answer. Esempio: Lei ha un giardino? (*yes*) **= Sì, ho un giardino.**

a Ci sono fiori nel suo giardino? (*yes*)
b Chi cura il giardino? (*you*)
c Ci sono alberi? (*a few*)
d Lei ha un orto? (*yes*)
e Preferisce curare il giardino o l'orto? (*the vegetable garden*)
f Che fiori preferisce? (*wild flowers*)
g La sua casa è antica o moderna? (*old*)
h Quante camere ci sono nella sua casa? (*three*)
i Quanti bagni ci sono? (*two*)
j C'è uno studio? (*no*)
k Il salotto c'è? (*There are two*)

PRATICA 2

 Using Pratica 1 as an example, practise (out loud) talking about your home: casa/appartamento, camere, giardino, orto...

LA FAMIGLIA FERRARI

Sulla veranda Chiara mostra all'amica l'album delle fotografie di famiglia.

Chiara	Questa è mia sorella Giovanna.
Francesca	Io non la conosco.
Chiara	Ci vediamo poco perché abita a Verona. Questa è sua figlia: mia nipote Lorenza. Questo è mio cognato. Lui è di Roma ma abita a Verona da molti anni.
Francesca	Vedo che hanno un bellissimo cane.
Chiara	Sì, hanno anche un gatto e un canarino (*canary*). La settimana prossima intendo andare a trovarli. Vuoi venire?
Francesca	Con piacere: ho bisogno di una vacanza e la settimana prossima sono in ferie (*on leave/on vacation*).
Chiara	D'accordo allora. Prendi qualcosa da bere?
Francesca	Ho voglia di un gelato: ne hai?
Chiara	Sì, è nel freezer. È arrivata un'auto: devono essere Roberto, Sergio e Valentina.
Francesca	Non passano molte auto qui. I tuoi vicini (*neighbours*) come sono?
Chiara	Sono molto simpatici: lei è una biuloga (*biologist*) di Pavia, è divorziata (*divorced*). Lui è vedovo (*widower*). È avvocato. *(to Roberto)* Hai portato la carbonella (*charcoal*) per il barbecue?

 TIP

Simpatico/antipatico: when expressing a general feeling towards a person, you can say: **Mario è simpatico/antipatico**.

If you wish to stress your own personal feeling, you can say: **Mario mi è simpatico/antipatico**.

Answer the questions in the same way as you did in Pratica 1.

a Lei ha fratelli e sorelle? (*a brother and a sister*)

b Quanti anni ha suo fratello? (*44*)

c E sua sorella? (*38*)

d Che lavoro fanno? (*Your brother is a biologist, your sister is a lawyer*)

e Lei ha animali domestici? (*a dog and a cat*)

f Quando va in ferie? (*on July 15, for three weeks*)

g Come sono i suoi vicini? (*They are pleasant*)

PRATICA 4

 Practise talking about your family: one by one, say how they are related to you (cousins, in-laws, etc.), if you see them often, if they have pets… say as many things as you can think of.

DIALOGO 3

 Dopo il barbecue le due coppie (*the two couples*) prendono il caffè e continuano la conversazione in salotto.

Sergio	Che tranquillità! Si sentono soltanto gli uccelli.
Chiara	Pensa che mia suocera quando viene qui non può dormire! Dice che qui è troppo tranquillo!
Francesca	Quando io sono triste preferisco essere in città.
Sergio	Triste? Tu non sei mai triste quando sei in campagna: ridi e scherzi tutto il giorno.
Francesca	È vero, io in campagna sto bene. Posso aiutare a lavare i piatti?
Chiara	Oggi tocca a Roberto!
Roberto	Sei sicura? Io li ho lavati ieri.
Chiara	È vero ma io ho stirato, spolverato, rifatto il letto…
Roberto	Va bene, ho capito: tocca a me!

 Extend your vocabulary. The Italian word for a dishwasher is **lavastoviglie**. The dictionary may also give you **lavapiatti**: this usually refers to the person who washes dishes in hotels and restaurants. The word for *crockery* is **(le) stoviglie** (plural in Italian); *cutlery* is **(le) posate** (also plural); **cucchiaio**, **forchetta**, **coltello** and **cucchiaino** are respectively *spoon*, *fork*, *knife* and *teaspoon*.

Test yourself

1 **How would you say the following in Italian?**
   a I am hot.
   b She is pleasant.
   c She is unpleasant.
   d He is tired.
   e He is right.
   f He is wrong.
   g I feel like an ice cream.
   h I need a holiday.
   i I am a widower.
   j I have a dog and two cats.

2 **How do the people in the pictures below feel?**

a Sono _____!   **b** Sono _____!   **c** Sono _____!

d Ho _____!   **e** Ho _____!   **f** Ho _____!

SELF CHECK

I CAN. . .
○   . . . talk about my family
○   . . . say what I feel
○   . . . describe my home
○   . . . compliment people

17 Che tempo fa?
What's the weather like?

In this unit, you will:
▶ *practise talking about the weather and beach activities.*
▶ *revise how to describe something (Unit 4).*
▶ *revise how to describe the things you do (Unit 9).*

CEFR: (A2) *Can describe everyday aspects of your environment.*

With the help of the vocabulary on the next page, you should be able to understand the following passage. First, read the following passage, trying to, after that, understand as much as you can, with the help of the vocabulary that follows. Then, listen to the recording, and answer the questions.

Il clima italiano *The Italian climate*

17.01 Il clima italiano è temperato ma con grandi differenze non soltanto tra Nord e Sud ma anche tra la costa e l'entroterra e tra la pianura e la montagna. Le **Alpi** attraversano tutto il nord dell'Italia e gli **Appennini** attraversano la penisola da nord a sud. In inverno nelle Alpi fa freddo e il clima è asciutto con precipitazioni nevose e piogge scarse. In estate fa piacevolmente fresco.

Nelle regioni dell'Appennino (eccetto la Calabria) gli inverni possono essere rigidi (molto freddi) con precipitazioni abbondanti di neve e pioggia. Nella **Pianura Padana** (*Po Valley*) la zona che include il Piemonte, la Lombardia e l'Emilia, il clima è freddo e umido durante l'inverno con nebbia e foschia, in estate è afoso. Nella **Riviera Ligure** e lungo la costa del Mar Tirreno l'inverno è mite e l'estate è calda e asciutta. In inverno il clima della **Costa Adriatica**, dal nord fino ad Ancona, è influenzato dalla **bora**, un vento freddo che viene dall'Europa Orientale. Da Ancona al Sud il clima è di tipo Mediterraneo. Anche le isole hanno un clima Mediterraneo.

17.02

1 Il clima italiano è uniforme?

2 Generalmente dove nevica in inverno?

3 Nella Pianura Padana il clima invernale è buono?

Il tempo *The weather*

17.03

Che tempo fa?	*What's the weather like?*
Fa bel tempo.	*It's fine.*
Fa caldo.	*It's hot.*
C'è il sole.	*It's sunny.*
Il cielo è sereno.	*The sky is clear.*
Fa cattivo tempo.	*It's bad weather.*
Fa freddo.	*It's cold.*
Il cielo è coperto.	*The sky is overcast.*
È nuvoloso (nuvola).	*It's cloudy (cloud).*
C'è un temporale.	*There's a storm.*
C'è la nebbia	*It's foggy.*
foschia	*mist*
Piove (pioggia).	*It's raining (rain).*
Grandina (grandine).	*It's hailing (hail).*
Nevica (neve).	*It's snowing (snow).*
precipitazioni nevose	*snowfalls*
Tira vento.	*It's windy.*
Lampeggia/Tuona.	*There's lightning/It's thundering.*
tempo umido	*humid weather*
una giornata afosa	*a sultry day*
C'è una leggera brezza.	*There's a light breeze.*
entroterra	*inland*
la pianura	*the plains*
asciutto	*dry*
scarso	*meagre, scarce*
Il mare è calmo/agitato/mosso.	*The sea is calm/rough.*
rigido/mite	*severe/mild*

DIALOGO 1

17.04 **Roberto e Chiara sono andati a fare un'escursione in montagna.**

Chiara	Che ore sono?
Roberto	Le quattro e mezzo. È meglio cominciare a scendere. Guarda laggiù (*look over there*): c'è un temporale che si avvicina (*it's approaching*) da est.
Chiara	Lo vedo: fra mezz'ora è qui. Grazie al cielo (*thank heavens*) ho l'impermeabile tascabile (*lightweight pocket mac*) nello zaino (*rucksack*).Tu hai il tuo?
Roberto	Sì. Se camminiamo di buon passo (*at a good pace*) fra mezz'ora possiamo raggiungere il rifugio (*mountain refuge*). *(after 20 minutes)*
Chiara	Comincia a piovere. Presto… Grandina! Aiutooooo…(*Help!*)!

PRATICA 1

Fill in the spaces to indicate the weather shown in the pictures.
Esempi: Il cielo è coperto. Grandina.

a Il cielo è _____.

b Il mare è _____.

c Tira _____.

d C'è un _____.

e C'è la _____.

f _____.

What is the opposite of the following sentences?

a Oggi fa molto caldo.
b Il cielo è coperto.
c Fa cattivo tempo.
d Piove.
e Il tempo è secco.
f La temperatura è bassa.

La spiaggia *The beach*

17.05

ombrellone (m.)	*beach umbrella*
bagnino	*lifeguard*
il costume (da bagno)	*swimming costume/bathing suit*
asciugamano	*towel*
cabina	*bathing hut*
pericoloso	*dangerous*
bandiera rossa	*red flag*
battigia	*waterline*
scottare	*to burn/scorch*
insolazione	*sunstroke*
aspetta un momento	*wait a moment*
occhiali da sole	*sunglasses*
la (sedia a) sdraio (f.)	*deckchair*
nuotare	*to swim*
abbronzarsi	*to tan*
sabbia	*sand*
fare il bagno	*to bathe*
palla	*ball*
Divieto di balneazione!	*No swimming!*

DIALOGO 2

 17.06 **Chiara e Francesca sono alla spiaggia con Valentina mentre Roberto e Sergio sono andati per funghi.**

Francesca	Devo andare a prendere l'asciugamano che ho dimenticato in cabina.
Chiara	Il sole scotta oggi, ma il mare è troppo agitato, è pericoloso fare il bagno.
Francesca	Infatti. Il bagnino ha detto che è pericoloso entrare in acqua oggi. C'è la bandiera rossa, che è segnale di pericolo.
Chiara	Certo. Vieni qui Valentina che ci sediamo sulla battigia, e facciamo un castello di sabbia.
Francesca	*(Francesca answers for Valentina, who is near her.)* Valentina dice che preferisce giocare a palla perché il castello lo ha già fatto ieri. Io sto un po' al sole perché voglio abbronzarmi, poi vado sotto l'ombrellone perché non vorrei prendere un'insolazione!
Chiara	Allora metto gli occhiali da sole e poi giochiamo. Va bene, Valentina? Che bel costume che hai oggi…

 As well as *weather*, **tempo** translates as *time*: **Non ho tempo** *I have no time*. **È arrivato in tempo** *He arrived on/in time*. In music, it means *beat*: **andare fuori tempo** *to miss the beat*. In the cinema, it can also describe a part of a film: **primo/secondo tempo** *first/second part*.

 17.07 **First, read the text below and try to fill in the blanks. Then listen to the recording to see if you are right. You can also check your answer in the Key.**

FERIE D'AGOSTO *AUGUST HOLIDAYS*

Il 15 agosto è la festa dell'Assunta (*Assumption Day*). **a** _____ festa è **b** _____ estesa (*extended*) ai giorni che precedono e seguono (*follow*) il **c** _____ 15 e si **d** _____ festa di Ferragosto. Dopo il Ferragosto tutti ritornano al **e** _____ e sulle **f** _____ ritornano gli ingorghi (*traffic jams*) e gli incidenti (*accidents*).

? Test yourself

1 Vero o falso? *True or false?*

  a Quando il cielo è coperto ci sono molte nuvole.
  b Quando fa molto caldo generalmente grandina.
  c Quando la temperatura è alta fa molto freddo.
  d È preferibile fare il bagno quando il mare è calmo.
  e Per nuotare è necessario andare in piscina o al mare.
  f La bandiera rossa indica che il mare è calmo.
  g Per abbronzarmi devo stare al sole.
  h Non devo fare il bagno se c'è il divieto di balneazione.
  i In Liguria il clima è mite.
  j La bora è un vento freddo che viene dal sud.

2 Match phrases a–e to phrases 1–5 to make complete statements.

a Quando il mare è molto agitato…	**1** allora vado sotto l'ombrellone.
b Non voglio stare al sole…	**2** è pericoloso nuotare.
c Vorrei abbronzarmi	**3** ma non c'è vento.
d Vorrei fare un po' di windsurf…	**4** ma non c'è sole.
e Vorrei affittare una sdraio…	**5** e un ombrellone per oggi.

SELF CHECK

I CAN. . .
. . . describe the weather
. . . talk about the beach and related activities
. . . explain things I do

18 *Il pieno, per favore*
Fill it up, please

In this unit, you will:

▶ *learn some basic motoring phrases, including asking for petrol.*

▶ *practise some expressions required in an emergency.*

CEFR: (A2) *Can ask for everyday goods and services.*

Listen to, or read, the passage below, then answer the questions. Some new words are similar to their English equivalents.

Autostrade e superstrade *Motorways and freeways*

18.01 La rete autostradale in Italia è lunga più di 5.000 chilometri. La natura del terreno, per la maggior parte montagnoso, richiede la costruzione di molti ponti e gallerie con il conseguente investimento di molti capitali. Prima di entrare in autostrada bisogna fermarsi al casello e ritirare il biglietto. All'uscita bisogna pagare il pedaggio. Il costo del pedaggio dipende dalla lunghezza del percorso (*length of the journey*). In alcune autostrade si può pagare con la carta di credito. Nella maggior parte delle autostrade, si può pagare il pedaggio con VIACARD, una carta magnetica che si compra ai caselli, nelle aree di servizio ed in certe banche ed uffici turistici. Si può anche usare il **Telepass**: un sistema telematico che consente di pagare il pedaggio senza fermarsi al casello. Questo consiste in un piccolo apparato applicato all'interno dell'auto che dialoga direttamente con le porte di entrata e di uscita. È necessario, dunque (*therefore*), fare attenzione (*pay attention*) e immettersi nella corsia giusta (*enter the right lane*): se si paga in contanti, per esempio, si entra dove c'è scritto **biglietti** e all'uscita bisogna passare dal casello dove c'è l'esattore (= la persona che prende i soldi). La velocità massima in autostrada è di 130 chilometri. Le superstrade sono strade simili alle autostrade che collegano le città tra loro, evitando i centri abitati. Nelle superstrade non si paga il pedaggio.

HA CAPITO? *HAVE YOU UNDERSTOOD?*

18.02

1 Il pedaggio si paga all'entrata o all'uscita dell'autostrada?
2 Si può pagare il pedaggio con la carta di credito?
3 Prima di entrare in una superstrada bisogna fermarsi?

Automobile/auto/macchina *Car*

18.03

Ue (Unione europea)	*EU (European Union)*
l'autovettura	*car*
noleggiare un'auto(mobile)	*to rent a car*
chilometraggio illimitato	*unlimited mileage*
il distributore di benzina	*petrol/gas station*
benzina senza piombo	*unleaded petrol/gasoline*
Il pieno, per favore.	*Fill it up, please.*
mancare	*to lack/be short of*
gasolio/diesel	*diesel fuel*
Ho un guasto alla macchina.	*My car has broken down.*
cambiare una gomma	*to change a tyre*
Ho una gomma a terra.	*I have a flat tyre.*
batteria	*battery*
il radiatore	*radiator*
Può controllare…?	*Can you check…?*
l'acqua/l'olio/le candele	*the water/the oil/the plugs*
pulire il parabrezza	*to clean the windscreen/windshield*
posteggiare/parcheggiare	*to park*
divieto/vietato	*forbidden/prohibited*
zona di rimozione forzata	*tow-away zone*
la rete	*network*
la galleria	*tunnel*
il casello/il pedaggio	*toll booth/toll*
la lunghezza	*length*
il viaggio	*journey, trip*
collegare	*to link*

evitare (evitando)	*to avoid (avoiding)*
la patente	*driving licence*
il sottopassaggio	*subway, underpassage*

DIALOGO 1

 18.04 **Roberto e un suo collega (*colleague*) vanno a Roma in auto per lavoro. Durante il viaggio…**

Roberto	Devo fare benzina.
Collega	C'è un distributore a circa due chilometri.
(The car stops at the petrol station.)	
Roberto	Il pieno. Può controllare l'acqua e l'olio, per favore?
Benzinaio	L'olio va bene. Manca un po' d'acqua.
(He tops up the water.)	
Roberto	Grazie. Quant'è?
Benzinaio	Cinquanta euro per la benzina.
Roberto	E per l'acqua?
Benzinaio	Per l'acqua niente. Aspetti un momento che pulisco il parabrezza.
Roberto	Grazie. Buongiorno.

  EMERGENZA *EMERGENCY*

18.05

Aiuto!	*Help!*
Permesso!	*Let me through!*
Presto!	*Hurry!/Quick!*
Attenzione!	*Look out!*
Guardi!/Ascolti!	*Look!/Listen!*
Chiami…	*Call…*
un' ambulanza/la polizia	*an ambulance/the police*
i vigili del fuoco/i pompieri	*the fire brigade*
pronto soccorso	*casualty department/first aid*
In caso di emergenza telefonare al 113.	*In the event of an emergency, telephone 113*

You stop at a petrol station.

You	*Ask the attendant to fill it up, please.*
Benzinaio	Super o gasolio?
You	*Say you want super.*
Benzinaio	*(Seeing that you've come a long way.)* Vuole un controllo all'acqua nel radiatore?
You	*Say no thanks, the water is OK; can he check the oil?*
Benzinaio	*(He checks the oil.)* L'olio va bene.
You	*Ask him if he can clean the windscreen.*
Benzinaio	Certamente. Ecco.
You	*Ask how much it is.*

PRATICA 2

You want to rent a car and you go to an autonoleggio.

You	*Say that you would like to rent a car.*
Impiegato	Che tipo di auto desidera?
You	*Say you want a small car.*
Impiegato	Una Seicento va bene?
You	*Say yes, a Seicento is OK and ask him if it has unlimited mileage.*
Impiegato	Sì. Chilometraggio illimitato.
You	*Ask him how much it costs per day.*
Impiegato	Quaranta euro al giorno.
You	*Ask him if the petrol is included.*
Impiegato	No. La benzina non è mai inclusa.

DIALOGO 2

 Un signore anziano è svenuto sul marciapiede (*pavement/sidewalk*) in una via di Firenze. Un gruppo di persone si forma.

Passante	*(to another passer-by)* Guardi! Quel signore è svenuto (*has fainted*)! Bisogna chiamare un dottore.
Dottore	Permesso! Io sono dottore. È meglio chiamare un'ambulanza.
Passante	Presto! Chiamate un' ambulanza.
	(an ambulance arrives)
Dottore	Portatelo (*take him*) al pronto soccorso.

PRATICA 3

 Read the following passage and answer the questions below.

Guidare in Italia *Driving in Italy*

In Italia si guida (*drives*) sulla destra ed è obbligatorio tenere in auto il triangolo (*warning triangle*) da usare in caso di guasto e il giubbotto catarifrangente (*high-visibility jacket*). Se si ha un guasto alla macchina si deve telefonare al numero 116, dire dove si è e dare il numero di targa (*number-plate*) dell'auto.

Dalla metà di ottobre alla fine di aprile è necessario tenere in auto le catene (*snow chains*) se si viaggia in località montane. Nei centri abitati la velocità massima è di 50 chilometri all'ora. I segnali stradali che indicano le autostrade sono verdi e il numero dell'autostrada è preceduto da A (per autostrada), per esempio l'A1 è l'autostrada Milano–Napoli; i segnali indicanti le strade statali (*A roads*) sono blu e il numero della strada è preceduto da SS (strada statale). La velocità massima nelle strade statali è di 90 chilometri all'ora.

Vero o falso? *True or false?*

  a In Italia è obbligatorio tenere il triangolo in garage.
  b È necessario avere le catene in estate.
  c La velocità massima in città è di 50 chilometri all'ora.

ASCOLTA E SCRIVI *LISTEN AND WRITE*

 18.06 **Listen to the dictation and write down what you hear. Then check your spelling against the passage above.**

? Test yourself

1 Can you say the following in Italian?

   a Fill it up, please.
   b Can you check the oil?
   c Can you change the tyre?
   d Quick, call the fire brigade!
   e I'd like to rent a car.
   f 10 euros of petrol.
   g 30 litres of diesel.
   h I have a flat tyre.
   i Can I park here?
   j Can you check the water level?

2 Someone calls for help: what does he/she say?

   a Presto!
   b Aiuto!
   c Guardi!

3 Someone is about to step on a banana skin: what do you say?

   a Ascolti!
   b Guardi!
   c Attenzione!

4 You run for the bus, but your Italian friend lags behind: what do you say?

   a Presto!
   b Aiuto!
   c Permesso!

SELF CHECK

I CAN. . .
. . . ask for everyday services
. . . know the language to use in an emergency situation
. . . can describe problems with my vehicle

Key to exercises and tests

Greetings **Ciao** means *hello* **and** *goodbye*

Vocabulary Builder *And you* (informal)? = **E tu**? *And you* (formal)? = **E Lei**?

Remo Ciao, Lucia! / *Lucia* Buongiorno, Remo! / *Lucia* Come sta? Come stai? / *Remo* Bene, grazie.

New Expressions **b** 5; **c** 1; **d** 6; **e** 4; **f** 2

Dialogues 1 Morning **2** Yes, very well **3** Not too well

Language discovery E Lei/Formal

Asking questions Prego

Practice **1 a** Buonasera, signorina. **b** Buongiorno, signora. **c** Buonanotte, signore. **2** Buonanotte **3** No, grazie **4 a** Scusi **b** Prego **c** Prego? **d** Parli più lentamente **e** Parla inglese? **5 a** Mi dispiace **b** Buonasera **c** Prego **d** Bene, grazie **e** Per favore **f** E Lei?

Test yourself **1** Scusi **2** Buonasera **3** Prego **4** Prego? **5** Mi dispiace **6** Bene, grazie. E Lei? **7** Parla inglese? **8** Parli più lentamente (per favore)! **9** Buonanotte, signor Bini **10** No/Sì, grazie.

UNIT 2

Review **1** Come sta? **2** Scusi? **3** Prego?

Language discovery The final 'e' of **dottore** is dropped when it precedes the first or surname.

Vocabulary builder **ti chiami** = *you are called*; **non** = *not*; **non sono** = *I am not*

Dialogues **1** Formal **2** Signora Pucci **3 a** Come si chiama? **b** Mi chiamo **c** No, non sono **d** E Lei, come si chiama? **5** No. She only speaks Italian. **6** Her name is Valentina, and she is Sergio and Francesca's daughter. **7 a** False; **b** False; **c** True; **d** False **8 a** 4; **b** 1; **c** 5; **d** 3; **e** 2

Language discovery Nostra figlia è ricca. Questo è nostro figlio.

Practice **1 a** James non parla italiano. **b** Non sono Francesca. **c** Non parlo inglese. **d** Valerio non è tedesco. **e** Il signor Lupi non è straniero.

2 a la **b** il **c** la **d** il **e** il **f** il **g** la **h** il **i** la **j** la   **3 a** il **b** a **c** o **d** la **e** il **f** a
4 a una **b** un **c** un **d** una **e** un **f** un **g** un **h** una **i** un   **5 a** Questo
b Questa **c** Questa **d** Questo **e** Questa **f** Questa   **6 a** tedesco **b** canadese
c portoghese **d** inglese **e** svizzera **f** gallese **g** austriaca **h** irlandese
i scozzese **j** americana **k** spagnolo **l** francese

Reading **a** *dear* **b** *husband* **c** *cat* **d** *we have* **e** *we live* **f** *soon* **a** *Jenny's*
son **b** *Wales* **c** *A dog* **d** *Yes*

Test yourself **1 a** Come si chiama?/Come ti chiami? **b** Lei si chiama...?/
(Tu) ti chiami? **c** Parla inglese?/Parli inglese?   **2** Chi è?; Buongiorno signor
Gucci, come sta?; Non c'è male, grazie. Si accomodi.; Questo è mio marito/
questa è mia moglie.; Piacere.

UNIT 3

Review **a** Chi è? **b** Grazie. **c** Parla inglese?

Language discovery **Venti** = 20

Vocabulary builder **dove** = *where*; **non capisco** = *I don't understand*;
piazza = *square* **lavoro** (m); **commessa** (f.); **negozio** (m.) **studio** (m.)

Dialogues **1** Nobody knows where via Mazzini is. **2** Francesca lives in
Genova. **a** False **b** False **c** True   **3** Francesca is married with a six-year-old
daughter.   **4** Sergio lives in Genoa at 15 Roma Street in the town centre
near Garibaldi Square.   **5** Brunella teaches maths.

Language discovery **Change the -o into an -i, so anni; Sono
cameriere** ; **Sono dentista**.

Practice **1 a** la **b** la **c** il **d** il **e** il **f** il **g** Non capisco.   **2 a** in **b** a **c** in **d** a **e**
in **f** a.   **3 a** È italiano? **b** Di dov'è? **c** Io sono (your name) e Lei, come si
chiama?

Test yourself **1** È sposato? **2** Ha figli? **3** Quanti figli ha?   **4** Che
lavoro fa?   **5** È italiano?   **6** Dove abita?   **7** Quanti anni ha suo figlio?
8 Lei lavora?   **9** Di dov'è?   **10** Scusi, dov'è (la banca/il teatro etc.)?

UNIT 4

Review **1** Mi chiamo (your name)   **2** Sono (your nationality)   **3** Abito
a... **4** Ho... anni.

Language discovery Un caffè, per favore.

Vocabulary builder **Di che colore è?** = *What colour is it?*; **C'è un
telefono qui?** = Is *there a telephone here?*; **Non c'è**... = *There is no*... ; **Ci
sono negozi qui vicino?** = *Are there (any) shops nearby?*; **il mio/la mia** =
my, mine

Dialogues **1** Because the tea is too weak and lukewarm. **2** Italian coffee is strong. **3** It's a lemon. **4** The opposite of large (grande) is 'piccolo' (small) and the opposite of cold (freddo) is caldo (hot). **5** No, there aren't any biscuits. **6** One is white, the other is red. **7** She likes some operas but not all.

Practice **1 a** Questa birra è fresca! **b** Questa strada è lunga! **c** Questo biscotto è dolce. **d** Questo caffè è molto caldo! **e** Questo gelato è molto freddo! **2 a** leggero **b** alto **c** anziano **d** lungo **e** pieno **f** piccolo **g** vecchio **3 a** Il limone è giallo. **b** La banana è gialla. **c** La carne è rossa. **d** L'erba è verde. **e** I limoni sono gialli. **f** Le banane sono gialle. **4 a** Cinque più sei fa undici. **b** Sette per dieci fa settanta. **c** Mille diviso cinque fa duecento. **d** Sei per sette fa quarantadue. **5 a, b, c:** Sì, c'è. **d, e, f:** Sì, ci sono. **6 a, b, c**: No, non c'è. **d, e, f**: No, non ci sono. **7 a, c, d, f, g**: No, non mi piace. **b, e, h**: No, non mi piacciono. **8 a** Sì, mi piace ma preferisco **i** biscotti. **b** Sì, mi piacciono ma preferisco le mele. **c** Sì, mi piace ma preferisco andare a teatro. **d** Sì, mi piace ma preferisco il tè. **e** Sì, mi piacciono ma preferisco le torte. **f** Sì, mi piace ma preferisco la birra. **g** Sì, mi piace ma preferisco il pesce. **h** Sì, mi piacciono ma preferisco la frutta.

Test yourself **1** Che cos'è questa? **2** È buono? **3** Qual è la sua auto(mobile)? **4** C'è l'acqua? **5** Ci sono i limoni? **6** Di che colore è il mare? **7** Le piace questo vino? **8** Le piacciono le mele? **9** Che cos'è questo? **10** Com'è il tè?

UNIT 5

Shopping **1** due edicole **2** una rivista **3** un biglietto

Vocabulary builder **1** Mezzo chilo di mele, per favore. **2** Un caffè e due cappuccini. **3** Il suo vino è rosso.

Dialogues **1** Brunella asks for a coffee and a roll. **a** False **b** True **c** False **2** Five euros a kilo.

Language discovery **Due euro al litro.**

Practice **1 a** C'è un supermercato qui vicino? **b** C'è una banca qui vicino? **c** C'è una farmacia qui vicino? **d** C'è un ufficio turistico qui vicino? **e** C'è una libreria qui vicino? **2 a** Devo andare in banca. **b** Vado in drogheria. **c** Devo andare dal fruttivendolo. **3 a** vorrei mezzo chilo di pomodori maturi; **b** vorrei cinque banane **4 a** Quanto costa un etto di prosciutto crudo? **b** Quanto costa un litro di latte? **c** Quanto costa mezzo litro di vino? **5** Quant'è in tutto?

Test yourself **1** Desidera altro? **2** Quanto costa? **3** Dove deve andare? **4** È caro? **5** Dove devo pagare? **6** Desidera? **7** Quanto costa un chilo di pane? **8** A chi tocca? **9** Com'è questo prosciutto? **10** Come vuole il panino?

UNIT 6

Review **a** dicias sette; **b** sette; **c** sei; **d** trentuno; **e** quarantotto; **f** dodici; **g** ventotto; **h** quindici; **i** cinque; **j** sessantasette; **k** settantasei; **l** tredici; **m** cento; **n** mille; **o** duemilacinquecentosettanta; **p** dodicimilatrecentoquarantasette; **q** venticinquemilaotto-centonovantuno

Shop opening hours **alcune pasticcerie**

Vocabulary builder **a** 4; **b** 3; **c** 1; **d** 2

Time expressions

questa sera (= **stasera**) = *this evening*; **Che giorno è oggi?** = *What day is it today?*; **dopodomani** = *the day after tomorrow*; **mezz'ora più tardi** = *half an hour later*

New expressions **è aperta** = *it is open*; **all'ora di pranzo** = *at lunchtime*; **alcune citta'** = *some towns/cities*

Parts of the day **a** la notte; **b** la mattina; **c** la sera

Writing dvoegìi = *Thursday*; codnieam = *Sunday*; obatsa = *Saturday*; lìmreodce = *Wednesday*; ìnelud = *Monday*; rdnvìee = *Friday*; etìmdar = *Tuesday*

The months of the year The months and days of the week in Italian don't take a capital letter.

Dialogues **1** Too early **2** 3.30 p.m.; no; half past four. **3** Garibaldi Square; yes; Ci vediamo.

Language discovery 6.40 p.m. (twenty to seven) (feminine because alcune has the feminine 'e' ending)

Practice **1 a** No **b** Sunday **c** Thursday 13 January at 9 p.m. **2 a** Scusi, a che ora apre la farmacia? **b** A che ora comincia lo spettacolo? **c** A che ora aprono i negozi la mattina? **3 a** domani mattina **b** dopodomani sera **c** ieri mattina **d** oggi pomeriggio **e** domani sera **4 a** Quando **b** è troppo presto **c** Quando **d** più tardi **e** chiusi

Test yourself **1** A che ora chiudono i negozi la sera? **2** C'è una farmacia aperta la domenica? **3** Nei giorni feriali, i negozi di generi alimentari sono sempre aperti? **4** I bar aprono la domenica? **5** I supermercati

chiudono il mercoledì pomeriggio? **6** Quanti giorni ha settembre?
7 Quando vai/va in vacanza? **8** A che ora finisce il film? **9** Quanto dura
lo spettacolo? **10** Che giorno è (oggi)?

Review 1 È troppo presto, i negozi aprono alle tre e mezzo. **2** A che ora
chiudono i negozi il sabato pomeriggio? **3** Quando finisce lo spettacolo?

Trains un viaggio

**Vocabulary builder A che ora arriva il treno? Il treno arriva alle
nove.**

**Tickets un biglietto di andata e ritorno; seconda classe; prenotare/
riservare il posto**; *to validate* (a ticket)

Dialogues 1 No, at 13:15 (quarter past one); No; Platform 1. **2** Como;
No, with her seven-year-old daughter.

Practice 1 Domani mattina; Andata e ritorno; No, prima; Sì, ecco.
2 a ferma in tutte le stazioni **b** va a Losanna **c** ferma a Parigi **3 a** Un
biglietto di andata e ritorno per Roma. **b** A che binario arriva il treno da
Genova? **c** Il biglietto è valido per due mesi. **d** A che ora parte l'InterCity
per Firenze? **e** Vorrei sapere l'orario festivo. **f** Va direttamente o devo
cambiare? **g** Il treno viaggia con alcuni minuti di ritardo. **4** Il prossimo
treno per Roma parte alle dieci e (zero) due; Bisogna cambiare a Padova;
La coincidenza è alle undici e arriva a Roma alle diciotto e trenta; No, è
un InterCity; Sì, bisogna prenotare il posto; Andata?; Due mesi; Prima o
seconda (classe)?

Test yourself 1 True **2** False **3** False **4** True **5** False **6** False

**Review Sì, viaggia con venti minuti di ritardo; A che binario arriva?;
Arriva al binario sette**.

The stroll passeggiare

Vocabulary builder 1 Vorrei andare al cinema. **2** Voglio andare in
campagna. **3** Preferisco stare a casa.

Comparisons and other useful vocabulary 1 ancora **2** comprare
3 mentre

Dialogues 1 Francesca is going to the supermarket, then to the
bookshop to buy a present. Lastly she is going to the theatre to look for
tickets for Aida. Sergio is going to visit Paolo on a work-related matter.
a False **b** True **c** False **2** The larger one

Language discovery 'La' refers to 'guida' which is feminine. **4 è più interessante**. **5 a buona b cattivo**

Practice **1 a** Io voglio andare **a** fare una passeggiata. **b** Io preferisco andare al cinema. **c** Io voglio andare al mare. **d** Io preferisco stare in città. **e** Io voglio andare a casa. **2 b** Bruno preferisce andare al cinema. **c** Giovanni vuole andare al mare. **d** Franco preferisce stare in città. **e** Barbara vuole andare a casa! **3** Voglio/Posso/Preferisco/Devo: vedere Maria; guardare la televisione; andare domani/a casa/a Roma; uscire domani; stare a casa/a Roma. **4 b** Ne ho una. **c** Ne prendo otto. **d** Ne voglio un etto/cento grammi. **e** Ne ho ventotto. **f** Ne ho due. **5 a** migliore **b** peggio **c** peggiore **d** di più **e** (di) meno **6 a** caro; più caro **b** meno cari

Test yourself **1** Qual è il migliore? **2** Quale mi consiglia? **3** Non voglio un vino dolce. **4** Voglio spendere (di) meno. **5** Preferisco questo. **6** Ne voglio tre litri. **7** La borsa più grande è migliore. **8** La carne costa più del pane. **9** Io parlo bene ma tu parli (or lei parla) meglio. **10** Le opere d'arte più interessanti sono a Firenze.

UNIT 9

Review **1** Dopodomani vedo Carlo. **2** Roberto parla piu' di Silvia. **3** Ne vendiamo tante.

Travelling by road Many 'imported' foreign words do not take a plural ending.

Vocabulary builder **Mi addormento tardi.** *I get to sleep late*; **Si diverte tantissimo.** *He/she enjoys himself/herself very much.*

Other useful vocabulary **a** 5; **b** 6; **c** 2; **d** 8; **e** 4; **f** 3; **g** 1; **h** 7

Dialogues **1** Only when something very interesting is on. **a** No; **b** Yes; **c** Tutti e tre. **2** Francesca gets up at 6.30am. **a** False **b** True **c** False

Language discovery **Non ci alziamo mai prima delle sette. Poi Umberto, il mio compagno, si fa la barba, e si veste. Beve un caffè e poi esce. Non mangia niente/mai al mattino.**

Practice **1** A che ora ti svegli la mattina?; E a che ora ti alzi?; A che ora esci?; Esci da sola?; Fate colazione insieme? **2** Chi prepara la colazione?; Valentina fa colazione con voi?; Valentina esce con voi: non è troppo presto per lei? **3 a** sveglia **b** alza **c** rade/fa la barba **d** veste **e** colazione **f** escono **4 a** sempre **b** mai **c** spesso **d** Qualche; altre **e** nessuno?

f nessuno **g** niente **h** qualcuno   **5 a** C'è nessuno? **b** Non conosco nessuno. **c** Va spesso per funghi? **d** Va mai in città?

Test yourself   1 a Si addormenta sempre tardi e non si stanca mai. **b** Si veste sempre male e non si pettina mai. **c** Parla sempre e non ascolta mai. **d** Guarda sempre la televisione e non lavora mai. **e** Si diverte sempre e non studia mai. **f** Sa sempre tutto e non ubbidisce mai. **g** Mangia sempre dolci e non si lava mai i denti.   **2 a** pacchi **b** amici **c** banche **d** psicologi **e** parchi **f** alghe **g** mucche

UNIT 10

Review   1 Grazia e Tommaso si svegliano alle otto meno un quarto. **2** Non conosco nessuno in questa città, però faccio una passeggiata in centro.   **3** Laura e le sue amiche escono sempre la sera, e vanno in discoteca.

Documents   molte leggi

Vocabulary builder   sono partito/a presto; **sono arrivato/a tardi**; **sono entrato/a nel negozio**; **sono ritornato/a a casa**.

Verbs taking avere   ho perso il treno; **ho perso il biglietto**; **ho dimenticato i passaporti**; **ho mangiato abbastanza**.

Dialogues   1 Francesca ha confermato la prenotazione la settimana scorsa. **a** False. He has already got them.   **2** Outside.   **3** Manuela didn't say if she'd been to the museum.   **4 a** Two hours; **b** A vase; **c** She's already eaten too much.

Language discovery   The past participle of verbs taking '**essere**' as an auxiliary must agree in number and gender with the subject.

Practice   1 a Mi sono alzato/a presto, **b** ho fatto colazione alle sette e mezzo/trenta, **c** ho letto un giornale italiano, **d** ho chiamato un tassì **e** sono andato/a al museo, **f** sono uscito/a dal museo, **g** sono andato/a in banca, **h** sono ritornato/a all'albergo.   **2** svegliati; sono alzato; sono andato; ho portato; sono lavato; sono vestito; sono alzata; sono lavata; sono vestita; ho svegliato   **3** No, siamo inglesi; Siamo arrivati questa mattina; No, questa è la prima volta; Di dov'è Lei?; Siamo stati a Firenze per una settimana; Sì, là fa troppo caldo così abbiamo deciso di venire qui. **4 a** specialmente **b** lentamente **c** normalmente **d** possibilmente **e** direttamente **f** terribilmente **g** chiaramente

Test yourself   1 a in appartamenti **b** No **c** Gli edifici vecchi/Quelli vecchi **d** No **e** Circa il ventisei per cento. **f** La seconda casa si trova al mare, in campagna o in montagna. **g** Durante il fine settimana e per le vacanze.

h Ogni giorno i residenti d<u>e</u>vono salire molte scale. **i** Ha aumentato la tassa sulla seconda casa. **j** No   **2 a** Delia ha preso l'autobus alle otto. **b** Dario e Mauro sono partiti ieri in treno. **c** La macchina viaggia troppo rapidamente. **d** Valentina mangia tante ciliegie. **e** I carabinieri si sono alzati molto presto.

UNIT 11

Have you understood?   **1** Carne; verdura; vino   **2** Sì   **3** L'abbigliamento

Wholegrain cereals   **1** In the external part   **2** Pesticides and chemicals   **3** Wholemeal cereals grown without pesticides

Dialogues   **1** Uova, carne, formaggio, funghi e or<u>i</u>gano   **2** Compra una lattina di Lavazza Oro. Vuole uova di giornata.   **3** Perchè sono pomodori nostrani freschissimi.   **4** C<u>o</u>mprano due magliette (una nera, una rosa).

Practice   **1** Che ripeno è?; Ne prendo due porzioni. Poi vorrei una porzione di pollo arrosto e una (porzione) di insalata di pesce. L'insalata di pesce è fresca?; La può incartare bene? Quant'è?; Ecco dieci <u>e</u>uro.   **2** Vorrei: **a** tre etti/trecento grammi di prosciutto non troppo grasso. **b** sei lattine di birra. **c** un pezzo di formaggio non troppo piccante. **d** mezza dozzina di uova di giornata. **e** una lattina/un pacchetto di caffè macinato. **f** un pacchetto/una confezione di piselli surgelati. **g** una scatoletta di pomodori pelati. **h** due etti/duecento grammi di burro.   **3 a** Patate, cipolle, fagioli, fagiolini, zucchini, carote, porri, zucca **b** Un gr<u>a</u>ppolo d'uva nera **c** I fagiolini sono nostrani? **d** Vorrei mezza zucca. **e** È tutto per oggi. **f** Mezzo chilo di panini integrali. **g** Questo pesce non è fresco; non lo voglio.   **4 a** Falso **b** Falso **c** Vero   **5** paio di scarpe; trentanove; c<u>o</u>stano; sconto

Test yourself   **a** scatoletta; **b** lattina; **c** piccante; **d** scatoletta; **e** bottiglia; **f** dozzina; **g** fresco; **h** pacchetto; **i** sacchetto; **j** Quant'

UNIT 12

Have you understood?   **1** Aeroporti, stazioni, nelle grande città e banche   **2** Dalle tre alle quattro/dalle quindici alle sedici   **3** No **4** Quella da 500 euro   **5** Un cent<u>e</u>simo

Dialogues   **1**   0044   **3** Il cambio è uno e cinquanta.

Practice   **1** Voglio fare una telefonata; Non ho il n<u>u</u>mero; Roma; Qual è il prefisso?; La linea è occupata/È occupato. Chiamo più tardi. **2** telefonata; n<u>u</u>mero; elenco tel<u>e</u>fonico; interurbana; prefisso; n<u>u</u>mero; occupato   **3 a** Mi dispiace ma tocca a me. **b** Des<u>i</u>dero spedire un espresso in Scozia. **c** Ha una busta? **d** Un francobollo per una cartolina, costa quanto un francobollo per una l<u>e</u>ttera? **e** Quanto costa un

francobollo per una cartolina per gli Stati Uniti? **4** Vorrei cambiare
duecento dollari USA in euro; Sì, ecco(lo); Hotel Pitosforo. Vorrei
anche cambiare un assegno turistico; Sì, quant'è il cambio oggi?;
Vorrei banconote di grosso taglio e cinque euro in spiccioli; Grazie,
buongiorno **5 1** b + f; **2** a +d; **3** c + e

Test yourself 1 a Dodici francobolli per la Gran Bretagna **b** Qual è il
numero di codice per Roma?/Qual e' il codice postale per Roma? **c** Il
mittente è necessario? **d** Avete/Ha un elenco (una guida) telefonico (-a)?
e Quant'è il cambio oggi? **f** Dov'è la buca delle lettere? **g** L'assegno è in
dollari o sterline? **2 a** Desidero inviare/spedire/mandare questa lettera
per posta prioritaria. **b** Vorrei cambiare questi dollari australiani in euro.
c Devo telefonare./Devo fare una telefonata. **d** Devo comprare un nuovo
caricabatteria per il mio cellulare. **e** C' è una presa vicino al tavolo?

UNIT 13

Have you understood? 1 No **2** All'ufficio turistico, in edicola, in
tabaccheria, e in alcuni bar **3** No, costa di più.

A ticket a 60 minuti; **b** 80 centesimi **c** Sì

Practice 1 fermata; all'altro lato; sinistra; lontano **2** Scusi, dov'è
il mercato del pesce?; Dov'è piazza Matteotti?; È lontano?; C'è una
libreria in piazza Matteotti?; No. Posso andare a piedi?; Dov'è la fermata
dell'autobus?; Molte grazie, arrivederla. **3** avanti dritto; seconda a sinistra;
altro lato della; giardini **4** Deve attraversare il ponte; Poi prende la prima
a sinistra e va avanti dritto. Alla fine della strada vede piazza San Marco.

Test yourself a Mi sono perso/a; **b** di fronte al duomo; **c** Deve tornare
indietro; **d** prima del porto; **e** dopo il semaforo; **f** dietro la stazione; **g** di
fronte alla panetteria; **h** sotto la torre dell'orologio; **i** vicino ai giardini;
j Posso andare a piedi?

UNIT 14

Have you understood? 1 Gli alberghi **2** No **3** No **4** No **5** No

Dialogues 1 Un albergo tranquillo e non troppo caro

Practice 1 a posizione panoramica **b** parco **c** ascensore **d** autorimessa
e piscina **f** posizione tranquilla **g** aria condizionata **h** telefono **i** televisore
j riscaldamento centrale **2** Buongiorno. Cerco un albergo in una
posizione tranquilla; Qual è il migliore?; Il Piccolo Parco va bene: può
telefonare per vedere se ci sono camere libere, per favore?; Voglio una
camera singola con doccia. **3 a** Per quante notti? **b** Quanto costa la

camera? **c** Va bene la patente?   **4 a** il conto **b** hanno fatto **c** un errore/
uno sbaglio   **5 a** La serratura non funziona. **b** La presa di corrente non
funziona. **c** Vorrei un'altra coperta. **d** Vorrei un'altra gruccia. **e** Non c'è
acqua calda. **f** Il radiatore non funziona. **g** La luce non funziona/Non
c'è luce. **h** Vorrei un altro cuscino.   **6 a** San Giorgio **b** 20% **c** No
8 a Domani mattina desidero la sveglia alle sei. **b** Dove posso
parcheggiare? **c** Può far portare **i** bagagli in camera?

Soggiorno in albergo vado; devo; devo; desidero; voglio; preferisco;
prendo; chiedo; voglio; arrivo

chiedo; posso; devo alzarmi; desidero; informo

Test yourself a Questa è la camera duecentonove. **b** Non c'è acqua
calda in bagno. **c** La doccia non funziona. **d** Ha una lista degli alberghi di
questa città? **e** Ha un posto per una roulotte? **f** Dov'è l'acqua potabile?
g Ha/Avete una camera doppia con bagno? **h** Dov'è la presa di corrente?
i Come si scrive il suo cognome? **j** Mi può dare il passaporto/i documenti?

UNIT 15

Have you understood? **1** Panini imbottiti   **2** Un 'tost'   **3** In autostrada
4 Cibo casalingo

Practice 1 Un tavolo per due; Possiamo sedere fuori?/Possiamo sederci
fuori?; Un analcolico e un succo di pomodoro senza ghiaccio.   **2 a** Con
il secondo piatto **b** Carni varie e verdure miste **c** No   **3** Che cos'è manzo
brasato con lenticchie?; Che cosa vuol dire/significa marsala?; La cotoletta
alla milanese è carne fritta?; Come si dice chop in italiano?   **4** Sì, grazie.
Salto l'antipasto; prendo zuppa di verdura e agnello arrosto; Come contorno
prendo carciofi fritti e patate arrosto; Il signore prende verdure ripiene e
pollo alla cacciatora con insalata; Mezza caraffa di vino rosso della casa e
mezza bottiglia di acqua minerale.   **5** Sì, grazie; Io vorrei la torta della casa
e per il signore del formaggio; Un digestivo, un caffè e il conto, per favore.

Test yourself a C'è troppo sale nella zuppa. **b** Vorrei del pane, per favore.
c Il pollo è freddo. **d** La bistecca non è ben cotta. **e** Non c'è pepe sul
tavolo. **f** Qual'è il piatto del giorno? **g** Vorrei spaghetti (ai frutti) di mare/
allo scoglio. **h** Preferisco acqua minerale naturale/non gassata. **i** Pesce alla
griglia, per favore. **j** Una bottiglia di vino bianco della casa, per favore.

UNIT 16

Have you understood? **1** Vero   **2** Falso   **3** Falso   **4** Falso   **5** Vero

Practice 1 a Sì, ci sono fiori nel mio giardino. **b** Io curo il giardino. **c** Sì, ci sono alcuni alberi. **d** Sì, ho un orto. **e** Preferisco curare l'orto. **f** Preferisco i fiori di campo. **g** La mia casa è antica. **h** Nella mia casa ci sono tre camere. **i** Ci sono due bagni. **j** No, non c'è uno studio. **k** Ci sono due salotti.

3 a Ho un fratello e una sorella.**b** Mio fratello ha 44 anni. **c** Mia sorella ha 38 anni. **d** Mio fratello è biologo, mia sorella è avvocatessa. **e** Ho un cane e un gatto. **f** Vado in ferie il 15 luglio per tre settimane. **g** Sono simpatici.

Test yourself **1 a** Ho caldo. **b** È simpatica. **c** È antipatica. **d** È stanco. **e** Ha ragione. **f** Ha torto. **g** Ho voglia di un gelato. **h** Ho bisogno di una vacanza. **i** Sono vedovo. **j** Ho un cane e due gatti.   **2 a** preoccupato **b** felice **c** triste **d** fame **e** freddo **f** sete

UNIT 17

Have you understood? **1** No   **2** Sulle Alpi e sugli Appennini   **3** No

Practice **1 a** sereno **b** agitato/mosso **c** vento **d** temporale **e** nebbia **f** Nevica **2 a** Oggi fa molto freddo. **b** Il cielo è sereno. **c** Fa bel tempo. **d** Non piove./C'è il sole. **e** Il tempo è umido. **f** La temperatura è alta.

Ferie d'agosto text: questa; stata; giorno; chiama; lavoro; strade

Test yourself **1 a** Vero **b** Falso **c** Falso **d** Vero **e** Vero **f** Falso **g** Vero **h** Vero **i** Vero **j** Falso **2 a** 2; **b** 1; **c** 4; **d** 3; **e** 5

UNIT 18

Have you understood? **1** All'uscita   **2** Sì   **3** No

Practice **1** Il pieno per favore; Super; No grazie, l'acqua va bene: può controllare l'olio?; Può pulire il parabrezza?; Quant'è?   **2** Vorrei noleggiare un'automobile; Voglio un'automobile piccola; Sì una Seicento va bene: ha il chilometraggio illimitato?; Quanto costa al giorno?; La benzina è inclusa?   **3 a** Falso **b** Falso **c** Vero

Test yourself **1 a** Il pieno, per favore. **b** Può controllare l'olio? **c** Può cambiare la gomma? **d** Presto, chiami i pompieri! **e** Vorrei noleggiare un'automobile. **f** Dieci euro di benzina **g** Trenta litri di gasolio **h** Ho una gomma a terra. **i** Posso parcheggiare qui? **j** Può controllare l'acqua? **2** b   **3** c   **4** a

REVIEW: UNITS 1–3

1 a Sono (your name); sono (your nationality); vengo da/sono di (your town). **b** Piacere. **c** Parli più lentamente, per favore. **d** (Lei) parla inglese, signora? **e** Io parlo inglese, tedesco e italiano. Sono insegnante. Sono sposato/a. **f** Dov'è la banca? **g** Dov'è Piazza Roma?

2 a la; **b** il; **c** il; **d** il; **e** la; **f** la **g** il; **h** il; **i** la; **j** l'.

3 a *Excuse me, where is the museum?* **b** *How old is the child/baby?* **c** *No, I'm not married.* **d** *I don't understand French.* **e** *I'm a foreigner.* **f** *This gentleman is very kind.*

4 a Le bambine; **b** I teatri; **c** Le pizze; **d** Le stazioni; **e** Le città; **f** I vini.

5 a Parliamo soltanto italiano. **b** Questo è il mio fratello. **c** Si chiama Pietro. **d** Abita in Svizzera? **e** Paola è commessa. **f** Caterina ha tre figli.

6 a Scusi, parla inglese?; **b** Marie-Claire è francese; **c** Una persona abita in Umbria; **d** Sono dentista; **e** Dov'è il parco?

7 Luigi abita in centro. Lavora vicino; e' insegna di geografia. Ha due cani Luigi non è sposato.

8 a Le figlie di Melania si chiamano Erica, Jessica e Lucia. **b** Queste sono le regioni d'Italia. **c** Mangio soltanto i cereali.

REVIEW: UNITS 4–6

1 *food* cibo: la carne; il pane; lo zucchero; la pizza; la pasta; il gelato; i biscotti; gli spaghetti; il prosciutto; il formaggio; il burro;
fruit frutta: le albicocche; il limone; le mele; la ciliegia; l'arancia;
drinks bevande: l'acqua; il latte; il tè; la birra; il vino; il caffè

2 a *You must pay at the cash desk.* **b** *Can we go to the supermarket tomorrow?* **c** *I prefer to go to the theatre.* **d** *I'd like two kilos of these.* **e** *Which is my ice cream?* **f** *My shoes are very expensive indeed.*

3 a siete **b** finisce **c** vedono **d** parte **e** costano **f** hanno **g** può

4 a duemilatrecentocinquanta **b** milleduecentonovanta
c cinquecentoquarantasei **d** un milione e settecentoquarantaduemila
e due virgola cinque

5 a Un caffè costa ottanta centesimi. **b** Mangia un panino. **c** Il totale è tre euro esessanta.

6 a 5; **b** 3; **c** 2; **d** 9; **e** 10; **f** 7; **g** 6; **h** 1; **i** 4; **j** 8.

7 a A che ora chiude la banca? **b** Qual' è il contrario di pesante? **c** Di che colore è la tua/Sua auto(mobile)? **d** Quant'è? e A che ora parti? **f** Quanto costa un chilo di mele? **g** Ti piace? **h** Che cos'è? **i** Ti piacciono? **j** Ci sono le torte? **k** Abita/abiti lontano dalla stazione?

8 a Vorrei andare a teatro stasera; **b** € 6,20 = Sei e venti; **c** In inverno fa freddo; **d** Ci vediamo alle dieci; **e** Mi piacciono gli spaghetti; **f** Gennaio è il primo mese dell'anno; **g** Matraia è una località vicino a Lucca; **h** Tutti gli studenti parlano italiano; **i** Al bar devi fare lo scontrino; **j** Questo vino è buonissimo!

9 a Il venerdì finisci il lavoro presto?; **b** La banca è aperta oggi?; **c** Vorrei un chilo di pomodori, per favore; **d** Qual' è il contrario di tiepido?; **e** Puoi andare dopodomani; **f** No, il museo è troppo lontano; **g** Mi piace il caffè ma preferisco il tè; **h** Ci vediamo al Bar Marisa; **i** Mi piace abitare/vivere in citta'; **j** Abbiamo trenta limoni.

10 a alimentari/drogheria; **b** fruttivendolo; **c** carne; meat; d pescheria;

11 a la posta/l'ufficio postale; **b** amaro; **c** quel negozio/quell'auto(mobile)-quella macchina/questa chiesa; **d** quegli studenti/questi ombrelli; **e** all'arrivo/al binario quattro/sul tavolo-sulla tavola; **f** Via Mazzini è stretta; **g** Questo treno è velocissimo; **h** I fratelli finiscono la birra

12 a Norma e Federico hanno un' automobile gialla. **b** Le mie scarpe rosse sono comodissime. **c** Di che colore è la tua automobile? **d** Mi piacciono queste ciliegie nere/Queste ciliegie nere mi piacciono. **e** Possiamo mangiare tutti i biscotti scozzesi?

REVIEW: UNITS 7–10

1

You	Buon giorno. Vorrei un biglietto per il prossimo treno per Venezia.
Impiegato	Il prossimo treno è un Eurostar. Va bene?
You	È/costa più caro degli altri treni?
Impiegato	Sì, ma è più veloce.
You	Va bene. A che ora parte?
Impiegato	Alle 09.37. Prima o seconda classe?
You	Seconda. Grazie. Devo convalidare il biglietto?
Impiegato	No, non i biglietti Eurostar / per l'Eurostar.
You	Bene. A che binario arriva?
Impiegato	Al binario 7. Buona giornata.
You	Grazie. Anche a Lei.

2 a li; **b** lo; **c** la; **d** le; **e** ne; **f** ne; **g** ne; **h** l'; **i** le; **j** l'/lo

3 a Il quattro dicembre; **b** Il primo maggio; **c** Il diciassette ottobre; **d** Il ventisei giugno.

4 Leonardo e Lucrezia lavorano di notte. Allora, si alzano alle cinque del pomeriggio. Lucrezia si lava prima di lui. Poi Leonardo si fà la barba mentre Lucrezia si veste. Fanno colazione insieme, e escono di casa alle otto di sera. Iniziano a lavorare alle dieci, e finiscono alle sei del mattino. Tornano e casa, fanno la cena, e si addormentano alle nove del mattino.

5 a *I've eaten very well indeed*; **b** *Did you meet in Spain?*; **c** *We went for a stroll in the park*; **d** *Madam, would you like to sit down?*; **e** *I never go out*

after midnight; **f** *My car is better than Luca's*; **g** *The coach usuallly arrives late*; **h** *Next week I'm going to the countryside*; **i** *I take two three times a day*; **j** *When I buy a magazine I read it immediately.*

6 a Si è alzata alle sei; **b** Si è fatta la doccia; **c** Si è lavata **i** denti; **d** Si è vestita velocemente; **e** Ha preparato il caffè; **f** Ha fatto (la) colazione; **g** Ha chiamato un tassì; **h** È uscita di casa; **i** È andata alla stazione; **j** Ha comprato un biglietto in seconda classe; **k** Ha preso il treno per Napoli; **l** Ha noleggiato una macchina; **m** È andata alla villa di sua sorella a Positano; **n** Ha cenato con sua sorella; **o** Si è addormentata presto

7 a False **b** True **c** True **d** False **e** True

8 a Ci svegliamo alle sette meno un quarto; **b** Gaia dice: Conosco Elena molto bene – siamo andate a scuola insieme; **c** Ugo ha molti animali, ma preferisce i gatti; **d** Milena parla molto dello sport; **e** Le bambine si sono pettinate per due ore!; **f** Perchè non venite mai a trovarci in Toscana?; **g** Oggi ho visto il film per la terza volta.

9 a al; **b** dei; **c** dal; **d** dalle; **e** dagli; **f** dei; **g** sul all'; **h** sul nel; **i** ai; **j** dal

10 a La mia borsa è più grande; **b** Eleonora è più giovane di Giampaolo; **c** Questo ristorante è il migliore a/di Siena; **d** (Lei) parla molto male il francese; **e** Il formaggio è cattivo ma la torta è peggiore; **f** Quel libro è più interessante di questo; **g** Grazie. Mio fratello sta molto bene; **h** Il pesce costa più della carne; **i** Clara è meno stanca di Samantha; **j** Il mio italiano è buono ma il mio portoghese è migliore.

11 a Quando ti alzi?; **b** Dove bisogna cambiare?; **c** Che cosa devi fare stamattina?; **d** Quando vuole viaggiare?; **e** Quanti figli hae come si chiamano **e** quanti anni hanno?; **f** Dove andate quest'estate?; **g** Ho bisogno del mio passaporto/mi serve il passaporto?; **h** Ti sei sbagliata?; **i** Vuoi sapere il risultato?; **j** A che binario arriva?

Italian–English vocabulary

This vocabulary is not intended to be comprehensive.

1 The English translations given apply only to the meaning of the word as used in the book.

2 Words ending in -o are to be considered masculine and those ending in -a feminine; in all other cases, the gender will be indicated (e.g. **mare** (m.), **automobile** (f.), etc.). Words with two different endings (e.g. **studente/essa; alto/a**) are nouns or adjectives with separate masculine and feminine forms.

3 Words ending in **-e** (e.g. **felice, dirigente**) with no indication of gender are adjectives or nouns suitable to both the masculine and feminine forms.

4 Verbs are given in their infinitive form (ending in **-are**, **-ere** and **-ire**).

abbastanza *enough, rather*
abbigliamento *clothing, clothes*
abito *dress; suit*
accettare *to accept*
accettazione *reception, check-in*
accomodarsi *to make oneself comfortable, to come in, to take a seat*
accordo *agreement;* **d'accordo** *OK*
accorgersi *to realize*
acqua *water*
adattatore (m.) *adaptor*
addirittura *even, actually*
addormentarsi *to fall asleep*
adesso *now*
affittare *to let, to rent, to lease*
afoso/a *sultry*
agitato *(sea) rough*
agosto *August*
aiutare *to help*

Aiuto! *Help!*
alba *dawn*
albergo *hotel*
albero *tree*
alcuni/e *some, a few*
alga *seaweed*
alimentare: generi alimentari *foodstuffs*
allegare *to enclose*
allora *then*
alto/a *high*
altro/a *other*
alzarsi *to get up, to rise*
amaro *bitter*
ambulatorio *surgery, doctor's office*
amico/a *friend*
ammettere *to admit*
ampio *wide-ranging, broad*
anche *also, too*
ancora *yet, again, still*

andare *to go*
animale *(m.) animal*
anno *year*
antico/a *old, antique*
anticipo *early (timetable)*
antipatico/a *unpleasant*
anziano/a *elderly*
appassionato/a *enthusiast, fan*
applicare *to apply*
appunto *note, memorandum*
aprile *April*
aprire *to open*
arancia *orange (fruit)*
arancio(ne) *(invariable) orange (colour)*
arbitro *referee*
area di servizio *(motorway) service area*
argomento *topic, subject matter*
aria *air*
arredamento *furnishing*
arrivare *to arrive*
arrivo *arrival*
ascensore *lift, (Am.) elevator*
asciugamano *towel*
asciutto/a *dry*
ascoltare *to listen (to)*
aspettare *to wait (for)*
assegno *cheque*
assortimento *selection, choice*
attendere *to wait (for)*
attraversare *to cross*
attualità *current affairs, topical subject*
aumentare *to increase*
autonoleggio *car hire, car rental*
autorimessa *garage*
autostrada *motorway, (Am.) highway*
autovettura *car*
autunno *autumn, (Am.) fall*
avanti *further on, forward*
avere *to have*
avversario *opponent*
avvicinarsi *to approach, to come nearer*

avviso *notice, announcement*
avvocato/essa *lawyer, attorney*
azzurro/a *blue*

bagaglio, bagagli *luggage, baggage*
bagnino/a *beach attendant*
bagno *bathroom;* **fare il bagno** *to swim; to have a bath*
bambino/a *child*
banca *bank*
bancomat *cash dispenser*
banconota *banknote*
bandiera *flag*
bar *bar (serving coffee, alcoholic drinks, snacks, etc.)*
barra *slash*
basso/a *low*
battello *boat*
batteria *battery*
battigia *waterline*
bello/a *beautiful, handsome*
benchè *although*
bene *well;* **benissimo** *very well*
benzina *petrol, gasoline*
benzinaio *service station attendant*
bere *to drink*
bianco/a *white*
bibita *drink*
bicicletta *bicycle*
bigliettaio/a *ticket collector*
biglietto *ticket; banknote*
binario *platform*
birra *beer*
biscotto *biscuit*
bisognare *to be necessary*
bisogno *need*
bistecca *steak*
blu *(invariable) navy blue*
bombola *gas bottle, cylinder*
bollito *boiled*
bora *bora (wind)*
borsa *handbag, (Am.) large purse*
bottiglia *bottle*
brasato *braised, braise*

bravo/a *good (at something)*

brezza *breeze*

bruciore *burning sensation*

brutto/a *ugly, (weather) bad*

buca delle lettere *letter box, (Am.) mailbox*

buffo/a *funny*

buonanotte/ buona notte *good night*

buonasera/ buona sera *good evening*

buongiorno/ buon giorno *good morning, (early afternoon) good afternoon*

buono/a *good*

busta *envelope*

burro *butter*

cabina *booth, kiosk, cabin*

caffé *coffee, bar (serving coffee, alcoholic drinks, snacks, etc.)*

cagna *bitch*

calcio *football, soccer*

caldo/a *hot*

calle *(f.) narrow Venetian street*

calmo/a *calm*

calpestare *to trample down, to tread upon*

cambiare *to change*

cambio *exchange bureau*

camera *room, bedroom*

cameriere/a *waiter, waitress*

camerino *fitting room*

camicia, camicetta *shirt, blouse*

caminetto *fireplace*

campagna *countryside*

campanello *doorbell*

campeggio *campsite*

campo *field*

calamaro *squid*

candela *spark(ing) plug; candle*

cane *(m.) dog*

capire *to understand*

capitaneria *harbour office*

capofamiglia *head of the family*

cappuccino *white coffee made with espresso machine*

carbonella *charcoal*

carciofo *artichoke*

carne *(f.) meat*

carnevale *carnival*

caro/a *dear, expensive*

carta (di credito) *(credit) card, paper*

carta d'identità *identity card*

cartello *signpost, notice*

cartolina *postcard*

casa *home, house*

casalingo/a *home-made; housewife*

casello *toll booth*

caso *case, event*

cassa *cash desk, cashier's desk*

cassetta small *letter box; mailbox*

cassiere/a *cashier*

categoria *class (of hotel), category*

cattivo/a *bad*

cellulare *(m.) mobile phone, cell phone*

cena *dinner, supper*

cenare *to have supper, to dine*

centesimi *cents*

cento a/one *hundred*

centralino *telephone exchange, operator*

centro *centre*

cercare *to look for*

cereale *(m.) cereal*

certamente/certo *certainly, surely*

cespo (di lattuga) *head (of lettuce)*

che *which, that, who, whom*

chi? *who?*

chiamare *to call;* **chiamarsi** *to be called*

chiaro *clear*

chiave *key*

chiedere *to ask*

chiesa *church*

chilo *kilo*

chilometro *kilometre*

chilometrico/a *kilometric(al)*

chiocciola *'at' sign (@)*

chiudere *to close, to shut*

chiuso/a *closed, shut*

ciao *hi, hello, bye bye, cheerio, so long*

cibo, cibi *food*

cielo *sky*

ciliegia *cherry*

cinema *cinema, (Am.) movie house*

cinquanta *fifty*

cinque *five*

cintura *belt*

cipolla *onion*

circa *about*

citofono *intercom, interphone*

città *town, city*

cittadino/a *citizen*

classe *(f.) class*

cliccare *to click*

clima *climate*

coda *queue, tail*

codice *(m.) code;* **codice di avviamento postale** *postcode, (Am.) zip code*

cognome *(m.) surname*

coincidenza *connection*

colazione *(f.) lunch; prima colazione breakfast*

colf (collaboratrice familiare) *home help*

collants *tights*

collega *(m. and f.) colleague*

collegare *to link, to join*

colore *(m.) colour*

colpa fault; essere in colpa *to be in the wrong*

come *as, like, how*

cominciare *to start, to begin*

commedia *play*

commesso/a *shop assistant, sales clerk*

comodo/a *comfortable, convenient*

compagno/a *companion, mate, partner, fiancé*

compilare *to fill in (a form)*

compito *homework*

compleanno *birthday*

completo/a *complete, included*

comporre il numero *to dial (the number)*

comprare *to buy*

compreso/a *included*

compressa *tablet*

comunicare *to communicate*

comunicazione *communication*

con *with*

condominio *condominium, joint ownership*

condomino *co-owner*

confermare *to confirm*

coniare *to invent, to coin a word*

conoscere *to know, to be acquainted with*

consegnare *to deliver*

consigliare *to advise*

contante *ready money, cash*

conto *bill, (Am.) check; account*

contorno *side dish/vegetables*

contrario/a *contrary, opposite*

contro *against, versus*

controllare *to check*

convalidare *validate*

convento *convent*

conversazione *conversation*

coperta *blanket*

coperto *overcast; (restaurant) cover charge*

coppia *couple, pair*

corrente *(f.) current*

corsa *(train, bus) trip, journey*

corso *course; avenue, main street*

corto/a *short*

cosa *thing*

così *so, thus*

costare *to cost*

costume da bagno *bathing suit*

cotto *cooked*

crudo uncooked

cucina cuisine, kitchen

cucinare to cook

curare to cure; to take care of

dappertutto everywhere

dare to give, dato given

data (indication of time) date

decimo/a tenth

denaro money

dente (m.) tooth

dentist dentist

dépliant leaflet, brochure

descrivere to describe

desiderare to wish

desiderio wish

destinatario/a addressee

destra right; a destra on the right

dettaglio detail

dettato dictation

dialogo dialogue

dicembre December

diciassette seventeen

diciotto eighteen

diciannove nineteen

dieci ten

difficile difficult

di fronte opposite

dietro behind

digestivo/a digestive, (after-dinner)
   liqueur

dimenticare to forget

dire to say, to tell; **detto** said, told

direttamente directly

diretto direct, through train

direttore/trice director, manager

direzione (f.) management

dirigente/direttore manager

diritto (law) right

discrezione (f.) discretion

dispiacersi to be sorry

distinto distinguished, different;
   (in letters) **distinti saluti** yours
   faithfully/sincerely

distributore (m.) vending machine;
   distributore di benzina petrol/
   gasoline pump

disturbo indisposition

divertimento amusement

divertirsi to amuse onself

dividere: diviso divided by

divieto prohibition

divorziato/a divorced; **divorzio** divorce

doccia shower

documento document

dodicesimo/a twelfth

dodici twelve

dolce (m.) sweet, cake

dollaro dollar

domanda question, request, application

domandare to ask

domani tomorrow

domenica Sunday

domestico/a domestic, household

donna woman

dopo after; **dopodomani** the day after
   tomorrow

doppio double

dormire to sleep

dottore, dottoressa (f.) doctor

dove where

dovere must, to have to; duty

dozzina dozen

dieci ten

dritto straight

drogheria grocer's (shop), grocery
   (store)

due two

dunque well then; so, therefore

duomo cathedral

durare to last

durante during

eccetto except

ecco here it is, here they are

ecologico ecological

edicola newspaper kiosk

edificio building

effettuare *to make, to carry out*
Egitto *Egypt*
elenco *list*, **elenco telefonico** *telephone directory*
elettronico *electronic*
emergenza *emergency*
entrare *to enter, to come/go in*
entroterra *inland*
epidemia *epidemic*
erba (aromatica) *herb*
errore *error, mistake*
esattamente *exactly*
esaurito/a *sold out*
espresso *express*
essere *to be*
est *east*
estate *summer*
estero *foreign*
esteso/a *extended*
età *age*
etto(grammo) *100 grams*
euro *euro(s)*
eurocity *fast trains linking various European cities*
eurostar *fast trains linking various Italian cities*
evitare *to avoid*

fabbrica *factory*
facchino *porter*
facile *easy*
facilmente *easily*
facoltà *faculty*
facoltativo/a *optional*
fagiolo *bean*
fagiolino *green bean*
falso *false*
fame *(f.) hunger*
famiglia *family*
familiare *(less common: **famigliare**) familiar, domestic*
fare *to do, to make*, **fatto** *made, done*
fare il numero *to dial (the number)*

farmacia *chemist's (shop), pharmacy, drugstore*
farina *flour*
farsi la barba *to shave*
favore *favour;* **per favore** *please*
febbraio *February*
felice *happy*
feriale: giorno feriale *working day*
ferie *(pl.) holidays, vacation*
fermare, fermarsi *to stop*, **fermata** *stop*
festa *public holiday; party*
festivo *festive, holiday*
fetta *slice*
fidanzato/a *fiancé(e),*
figlio/a *son, daughter*
fila *row; queue, line*
fine *(f.) end*
finestra *window*
finire *to finish, to end*
fiore *(m.) flower*
firmare *to sign*
focaccia *flat bread or cake*
forma *shape, form*, **una forma di formaggio** *a whole cheese*
formare *to form, to take shape*
formattazione *formatting*
formulario *form*
forno *oven*
forse *perhaps*
foschia *mist*
fra *between, among*
francobollo *stamp*
fratello *brother*
freddo/a *cold*
frequentare *to attend, to frequent*
fresco/a *cool, fresh*
fretta *hurry*
frigo *fridge*
fritto/a *fried*
frutta *fruit*
fruttivendolo/a *greengrocer*
fumare *to smoke*

funzionare *to work, to function*
fuoco *fire*
fuori *outside*

gabinetto *toilet*
galleria *tunnel, (theatre) circle*
gara *race*
gasolio *diesel*
gassato/a *(drink) sparkling*
gatto/a *cat*
gelato *ice cream*
generale *general*
generalmente *generally*
genere *(m.) kind, type*
genitore *parent*
gennaio *January*
gentile *kind, polite*
gestire *to run, to manage*
gettone *(m.) token, counter*
ghiaccio *ice*
giallo/a *yellow*
giardiniere *gardener*
giardino *garden*
giglio *lily*
giocare *to play*
giornale *newspaper*
giornaliero/a *daily*
giornata, giorno *day*
giovane *young*
giovedì *Thursday*
gioventù *youth*
girare *to turn*
giro *tour*
giugno *June*
giusto *just, correct, right*
gli *the (m. pl. before **z, ps, gn, pn** and **s** followed by consonant)*
goccia *drop*
godere *to enjoy*
gola *throat*
gomma *tyre; rubber*
gonna *skirt*
grammo *gram*

grana padano *a kind of parmesan cheese*
grande *large, big,* **grande magazzino** *department store*
grandinare *to hail,* **grandine** *(f.) hailstone*
granturco *maize*
grappolo *bunch (of grapes)*
gratuito/a *free of charge*
grazie *thank you*
grigio/a *grey*
griglia *grill,* **alla griglia** *grilled*
grissino *crisp breadstick*
grosso *large, (sea) rough*
grosso taglio *(banknote) large denomination*
guardare *to look at*
guasto/a *out of order, broken down*
guida *guide, (telephone) directory*
guidare *to drive*
gusto *taste*

i *the (m. pl.)*
idea *idea*
ieri *yesterday*
il *the (m. sing.)*
illimitato/a *unlimited*
imbarcazione *boat, craft*
imbottito/a *(roll) filled, stuffed*
immaginare *to imagine*
impacco *compress*
impanare *to cover with bread crumbs*
imparare *to learn*
impegnarsi *to commit, to undertake, to take it upon*
impermeabile *(m.) raincoat, waterproof*
impiegato *clerical/office worker*
in *in, at, to*
incartare *to wrap*
incassare *to cash*
incidente *(m.) accident*
incluso/a *included*
incontrare *to meet*

incoraggiare *to encourage*
indicare *to show, to point out*
indice di ascolto *audience rating*
indietro: tornare indietro *to go back*
indirizzo *address*
indisposizione *(f.) slight ailment*
infermiere/a *nurse*
informare *to inform*
informatica *computer science*
informatichese *computer language*
ingegnere *graduate engeneer*
ingorgo *(traffic) jam*
ingresso *entrance*
iniezione *(f.) injection*
iniziare *to start, to begin*
inoltre *also, besides, moreover*
inquilino *tenant, lodger*
insalata *salad*
insegnante *teacher*
insegnare *to teach*
insetto *insect*
insieme *together*
insolazione *sunstroke*
integrale *integral; (bread) wholemeal*
interessante *interesting*
intero/a *whole*
interregionale *interregional*
interrotto/a *interrupted*
interurbana *(telephone) long-distance call*
inverno *winter*
inviare *to send*
irritato/a *irritated*
iscriversi *to enrol*
iscrizione *enrolment*
isola *island*
italiano/a *Italian*

l' *the (f. sing. before vowel)*
la *the (f. sing.)*
là *there*
laggiù *over there, down there*
lampeggiare *to flash (lightning)*
lampo *lightning*

lampone *(m.) raspberry*
lana *wool*
largo *wide*
lasciare *to leave; (allow) to let*
lato *side*
latte *milk*
lattina *tin, can*
lattuga *lettuce*
laureato/a *graduate*
lavare *to wash,* **lavarsi** *to wash oneself*
lavorare *to work*
lavoro *work*
le *the (f. pl.)*
legge *(f.) law*
leggere *to read*
leggero/a *light, mild, weak*
lei *she, you (formal); her*
lentamente *slowly*
lento/a *slow*
lettera *letter*
letto *bed*
lezione *(f.) lesson*
libero *vacant, free*
libreria *bookshop*
libro *book*
limone *lemon*
linea *line*
lingua *language; tongue*
lista *list*
lo *the (before z, ps, gn and s followed by consonant)*
località *place, (holiday) resort*
locanda *inn*
loggione *(m.) gallery (theatre)*
lontano *far, remote*
loro *their, il, la, i, le loro theirs*
luglio *July*
lui *he; him*
luna *moon*
lunedì *Monday*
lunghezza *length*
lungo/a *long*
lungomare *(m.) seafront, promenade*

luogo *place,* **ha luogo** *takes place*
lusso *luxury*

ma *but*
macchina *car, machine*
macelleria *butcher's (shop)*
macinare *to grind, to mill*
madre *mother*
magazzino *store,* **grande magazzino**
   department store
maggio *May*
maggioranza *majority*
maggiorato *increased*
maglia *jersey, sweater*
maglietta *T-shirt, jumper*
mai *never, ever*
maiale *pork, pig*
malattia *illness*
male *(m.) badly; illness, ache,* **sentirsi**
   male *to feel ill*
mamma *mummy, mommy, mama*
mancare *to be lacking*
mancia *tip*
mandare *to send*
mangiare *to eat*
mantenersi *to keep (oneself);*
   mantenersi in forma *to keep fit*
manzo *beef*
marciapiede *sidewalk, pavement*
mare *sea*
marrone *(invariable) brown*
martedì *Tuesday*
marzo *March*
massimo: al massimo *at the most*
matrimoniale *(of bed) double bed*
mattina *morning*
maturo/a *ripe*
medio/a *medium*
medicazione *medication*
medicina *medicine*
medico *physician*
meglio *better*
mela *apple*
meno *less, minus*

mentre *while*
mercato *market*
mercoledì *Wednesday*
merenda *snack, afternoon tea*
meridionale *southern*
mese *(m.) month*
messaggio *message*
metà *half, middle*
mettere *to put;* **mettere il muso** *to*
   pull a face
mezzanotte *midnight*
mezzo *half, middle*
mezzogiorno *midday*
migliorare *to improve*
migliore *better*
miliardo (mille milioni) *thousand*
   million, billion
milione *(m.) million*
mille *(pl.)* **mila** *thousand*
minerale *mineral*
ministero *ministry*
minuto *minute*
il mio, la mia, i miei, le mie *my; mine*
misto/a *mixture*
mite *mild (climate)*
mittente *(m.) sender's address*
mobbing *a form of harassment carried*
   out towards a person in the workplace
   by his/her employer or colleagues.
mondo *world*
modello *style, type*
moderato/a *moderate*
modico/a *reasonable, moderate*
modulo *form*
moglie *wife*
molto/a *much, many, very, a lot*
momento *moment*
monastero *monastery*
mondo *world*
moneta *coin, money*
montagna *mountain*
mosso/a *(sea) rough*
mostrare *to show*

moto ondoso *wave motion*
motoscafo *motorboat*
mucca *cow*
multa *fine*
museo *museum*
musica *music*
muso *face,* **mettere il muso** *to pull a face*

nazionalità *nationality*
nebbia *fog*
necessario/a *necessary*
negozio *shop*
negoziante *shopkeeper*
nero/a *black*
nessuno *nobody*
neve *snow,* **nevicare** *to snow*
niente *nothing*
nipote *(m./f.) grandchild, grandson, granddaughter*
no *no*
non *not*
nono/a *ninth*
noia *nuisance*
noleggiare *to hire*
nome *(m.) name, first name*
nord *north*
il nostro, la nostra, i nostri, le nostre *our; ours*
nostrano *home-grown, locally produced*
nota *note*
notizia *piece of news*
notte *night*
novanta *ninety*
nove *nine*
novembre *November*
numero *number*
nuotare *to swim,* **nuoto** *swimming*
nuovo/a *new*
nuvola *cloud,* **nuvoloso** *cloudy*
nuvolosità *cloudiness*

obbligatorio *compulsory, obligatory*
obliteratore/trice *obliterator*

occhio *eye*
occhiali *glasses*
occupato *engaged, busy*
oggi *today*
ogni *every, each*
olio *oil*
oliva *olive*
oltre (a) *besides, as well as; beyond*
ombrello *umbrella,* **ombrellone** *beach umbrella*
omelette *omelette*
onesto/a *honest*
opera *work, opera*
operaio/a *labourer, workman/woman*
operatore *operator*
opposto *opposite*
oppure *or*
ora *hour, now*
orario *timetable, schedule*
ordinare *to order*
orologio *clock, watch*
orto *vegetable garden*
ospedale *(m.) hospital*
ospite *guest*
osteria *eating place, tavern, wine shop*
ottanta *eighty*
ottavo/a *eighth*
otto *eight*
ottobre *October*
ovest *west*

pacchetto *packet*
pacco *parcel, package*
padre *father*
paese *(m.) country, village*
pagare *to pay,* **pagamento** *payment*
pagnotta *loaf (of bread)*
paio *(pl.)* **paia** *pair*
palazzo *building, palace*
palestra *gymnasium*
palla *ball*
pane *bread*
panetteria *bakery*
panino *roll*

paninoteca *shop selling filled rolls and sandwiches*

pantaloni *trousers, (Am.) pants*

parabrezza *windscreen, (Am.) windshield*

parcheggiare *to park*

parcheggio *car park, (Am.) parking lot*

parco *park*

pareggiare *to draw*

Parigi *Paris*

parlare *to speak, to talk*

partenza *departure*

partire *to leave, to depart*

partita *match*

passante *passer-by*

passaporto *passport*

passato *past, bygone*

passare *to pass, to spend (time)*

passeggiata *walk, stroll*

passione *passion*

passo *pace, stride*

pasta *pastry, pasta, dough*

pasticca *lozenge*

patata *potato*

pasto *meal*

patente *(f.) driving licence*

peccato *pity*

pedaggio *toll*

peggio, peggiore *worse*

pelati (pomodori) *peeled (tomatoes)*

pelle *(f.) skin, leather*

pensare *to think*

penna *(f.) pen*

pensione *(f.) boarding house*

per *for*

perchè *because, why*

percorso *route, way, course*

perdere *to lose; to miss (e.g. a bus)*

pericoloso *dangerous*

periodo *period*

permettere *to allow, to permit, to let,* **permesso:** *let me through; allowed*

però *but, however, nevertheless*

pepe *pepper*

pesca *peach (also: fishing)*

pesce *fish*

pescheria *fishmonger's (shop), fish market*

pesante *heavy*

pettinarsi *to comb one's hair*

pezzo *piece*

piacere *to please,* **mi piace** *I like*

piano *floor, storey*

pianura padana *Po Valley*

piatto *dish*

piazza *square*

piccante *piquant, spicy, pungent, hot*

piccolo/a *small*

piede *(m.) foot*

pieno/a *full,* **fare il pieno** *to fill up (the tank)*

pillola *pill*

pioggia *rain*

piombo *lead*

piove *it's raining*

piscina *swimming pool*

pisello *pea*

più *plus, more, ...er*

piuttosto *rather, fairly*

pizzeria *pizza restaurant*

platea *stalls*

poco/a *little, few,* **un poco/un po'** *a little*

poi *then, later (on)*

polizia *police*

pollo *chicken*

poltrona *(theatre) stall*

pomata *ointment*

pomeriggio *afternoon*

pomodoro *tomato*

pompiere *(m.) fireman*

ponte *(m.) bridge*

pontile d'imbarco *jetty*

porgere *to give, to express*

porro *leek*

porta *door*

portare *to carry*

portiere *(hotel) porter, concièrge; (sport) goalkeeper*

portineria *(hotel) reception, front desk*

porto *harbour, port*

porzione *(f.) portion*

posate *(f. pl.) cutlery*

possedere *to own*

posta *mail, post office*

posteggiare *to park*

posto *place, seat*

potabile *drinkable*

potere *can, to be able to*

pranzare *to (have) lunch,* **pranzo** *lunch*

pratica *practice*

precedere *to go/come before, precede*

precipitazione *precipitation, (weather) rain*

preferire *to prefer*

prefisso *(dialling) code*

prego *don't menton it,* **prego***? pardon?*

pregare *to pray*

prelevare *to withdraw*

prelevamento *withdrawal*

prendere *to take; to catch*

prenotare *to book*

prenotazione *(f.) booking*

preoccupato *worried*

preparazione *(f.) preparation*

preparare *to prepare*

presa *(electric) socket*

prescrivere *to prescribe,* **prescritto** *prescribed*

presto *early,* **presto!** *hurry!*

previsione *forecast*

prezzo *price*

primavera *spring*

primo/a *first*

principale *main*

problema *(m.) problem*

professore/essa *professor, teacher*

promemoria *(m.) memorandum/ memoranda*

pronto *ready, (telephone) hello*

pronto soccorso *accident and emergency, casualty department; first aid*

(a) proposito *by the way, apropos of, with regard to*

prosciutto (cotto) *ham,* **(crudo)** *Parma ham*

proverbio *proverb*

proprio/a *own*

prossimo/a *next*

pubblicitario/a *promotional, advertising*

pubblico *public*

pulire *to clean*

pulito *clean*

pullman *(m.) coach*

punto *dot, point*

puntura *sting, bite*

purtroppo *unfortunately*

quadro *painting, square*

qualche *some, a few, any*

qualcosa *something*

qualcuno *someone*

quale *which*

qualità *quality*

quando *when*

quanto *how much*

quaranta *forty*

quarto/a *forth*

quattordici *fourteen*

quattro *four*

quello/a *that*

questo/a *this*

qui *here*

quindi *therefore*

quindici *fifteen*

quinto/a *fifth*

radersi *to shave*

radiatore *(m.) radiator*

ragazzo *boy,* **ragazza** *girl*

ragione *(f.) reason,* **aver ragione** *to be right*

rappresentazione *(f.) show, performance*

raro/a *rare*

il Redentore *the Redeemer*

regalo *present*

regata *regatta*

regionale *regional*

regolamento *rule, regulation*

restare *to stay, to remain*

resto *(of money) change*

rete *(f.) net, web*

riaprire *to reopen, to open again*

ricco *rich*

ricezione *reception*

richiamare *to call again*

richiedere *to require*

ricordare *to remember*

ridere *to laugh*

ridotto/a *reduced*

riduzione *(f.) reduction*

rifare *to do/make again*

riflettere *to reflect*

rifugio *refuge*

rigido/a *(of weather) severe*

rimborso *refund*

rimedio *remedy, cure*

rimozione forzata *illegally parked vehicles will be towed away*

ripieno *filling*

riscaldamento *heating*

riservare *to reserve*

rispondere *to answer*

risposta *answer*

ristorante *restaurant*

ritardo *delay*

ritirare *to withdraw*

ritornare *to return*, **ritorno** *return*

riva *shore*

rivista *magazine*

rivolgersi (a) *to turn/apply/speak/go to/ to address somebody*

rosa *(invariable) pink*

rosso/a *red*

rosticcere *owner of a roast-meat shop*

rosticceria *take-away/roast-meat shop*

roulotte *caravan, trailer*

rovescio *(weather) downpour*

sabato *Saturday*

sabbia *sand*

sacchetto (di plastica) *carrier bag*

sala *room*, **sala da pranzo** *dining room*

salame *salami sausage*

sale *salt*

salire *to go/come up*, **salire sull'autobus** *to get on the bus*

salotto *sitting room*

salsiccia *sausage*

saltare *to skip*

salutare *to greet*

saluto *greeting*

salute *(f.) health*

salve *hello, hi*

salvia *(herb) sage*

sangue *(m.) blood*

sapere *to know*

satellite *(m.) satellite*

sbagliarsi *to be mistaken*, **sbaglio** *mistake*

scala *stairs, staircase*

scarpa *shoe*

scarso/a *scarce, meagre, lacking (in), scanty*

scatola *box*; **in scatola** *tinned/canned*

scatoletta *tin, can*

scelta *choice*

scena *scene*

scendere *to go/come down*, **scendere dal treno** *to get off the train*

scheda *card*

scherzare *to joke*

scialle *(m.) shawl*

sciare *to ski*

sciarpa *scarf*

sciroppo *cough mixture, syrup*

scolaro/a *pupil, schoolboy/girl*

scomparire *to disappear*

scontento/a *dissatisfied, displeased*

sconto *discount*

scontrino *receipt*

scorso/a *(night, week, month, etc.) last*

scottare *to burn, scorch;* **scottatura** *burn, scald*

scrivere *to write*

scuola *school*

scuro/a *dark*

scusarsi *to excuse oneself,* **scusi, scusa** *excuse me*

sdraia *deckchair*

sedia a sdraio *deckchair*

secondo/a *second;* **secondo** *me in my opinion*

secco *dry*

sedere, sedersi *to sit*

sedici *sixteen*

segretario/a *secretary*

segreteria *secretary's office;* **segreteria telefonica** *answering machine*

seguire *to follow*

sei *six*

semaforo *traffic lights*

semplice *simple; single (journey)*

sempre *always*

sentiero *path*

sentire *to hear, to feel*

senza *without*

sera *evening*

sereno/a *cloudless, clear*

servire *to serve;* **servizio** *service*

sessanta *sixty*

sesto/a *sixth*

seta *silk*

sete *(f.) thirst*

settanta *seventy*

sette *seven*

settembre *September*

settentrionale *northern*

settimana *week*

settimo/a *seventh*

sì *yes*

sia... sia.../sia... che... *both... and...*

sicuro/a *safe, sure, certain*

significare *to mean, to signify*

signora *madam, lady, Mrs, Ms.*

signore *sir, gentleman;* **signor** *Mr.*

signorina *miss, young lady, Ms*

simbolo *symbol*

simpatico/a *nice, pleasant*

singolo/a *single*

sinistra *left*

sito *site*

soccorso *aid, assistance;* **pronto soccorso** *casualty, accident and emergency*

soldi *(pl.) money*

soggiorno *stay;* **luogo di soggiorno** *vacation resort*

sole *(m.) sun*

solito/a *usual,* **di solito** *usually*

solo/a *alone, lonely; only;* **da solo/a** *by oneself*

soltanto *only*

somma *sum*

sorella *sister*

sospeso/a *suspended*

sostanzioso/a *substantial*

sottaceti *pickles*

sotto *under*

sottopassaggio *subway, underpass*

spalti *(m. pl) (stadium) terraces, bleachers*

spazzino *road sweeper, street sweeper*

specchio *mirror*

specializzato/a *specialized*

spedire *to send*

spesa *shopping, expense, expenditure*

spesso *often*

Spettabile (Spett.) ditta *(commercial) Dear Sirs*

spettacolo *show, performance*

spiaggia *beach*

spicciolo *(small) change*

spiegare *to explain*

spolverare *to dust*

sporco/a *dirty*

sportello *(office) counter, (station) ticket window*

sposato/a *married*

spot *commercial spot*

spremuta *fresh fruit juice*

spuntino *snack*

squadra *team*

stagionato/a *mature, seasoned*

stagione *(f.) season*

stamattina *this morning*

stanco/a *tired*

stare *to stay*, **stato/a** *stayed, been*

stasera *this evening, tonight*

stazione *(f.) station*

sterlina *pound (sterling)*

stesso/a *same*

stirare *to iron*

stomaco *stomach*

storico/a *historic(al)*

strada *street, road*

straniero/a *foreign, foreigner*

stretto/a *tight, narrow*

studente/essa *student*

studiare *to study*

studio *study*

subito *at once*

succo *juice*

(il) suo, (la) sua, (i) suoi, (le) sue *his, her, hers, your (formal), yours (formal)*

supermercato *supermarket*

superstrada *motorway, expressway*

supplemento *surcharge*

supposta *suppository*

surgelato/a *frozen*

svegliarsi *to wake up*

sveglio/a *awake*

svendita *sale*

svenire *to faint, to pass out*

svestirsi *to undress*

tabaccheria *tobacconist's (shop)*

taglia *(clothes) size*

taglio *cut; (banknote) denomination*

tardi *late*

targa *number-plate, licence plate*

tariffa *(transport) fare, tariff, rate*

tascabile *pocket-sized*

tassa *tax, (custom) duty, (univ.) fee*

tasso *rate*

tavolo *table*

tazza *cup*

tè *tea*

teatro *theatre*

tedesco *German*

telefonare *to telephone*

telefonata *(telephone) call*

telefonista *operator, telephonist*

telefonino *mobile phone, cell phone*

telefono *telephone*

teleselezione *(f.) STD, direct dialling system*

televisione *television*

televisore *(m.) television set*

tempo *weather, time*

temporale *(m.) storm*

tenda *tent*

tenore *(m.) tenor*

termine *end, conclusion; term, period; deadline*

terra: una gomma a terra *a flat tyre*

terreno *land, ground*

terzo/a *third*

testa *head*

testare *to test*

(il) ticket *prescription charge*

tiepido *lukewarm*

tifo *(sport)* **fare il tifo per** *to be a fan of, to support*

tigre *(f.) tiger*

timbrare *to stamp*

tipo *type, kind*

tirare: tira vento *it's windy*

toccare *to touch*

tonno *tuna*

tornare *to return*

torre *(f.) tower*

tosse *(f.) cough*

torta *cake, tart, flan*

torto: avere torto *to be wrong, fault*

totale *total*

tra *between, among*

tramezzino *sandwich*

tramonto *sunset*

tranquillo/a *calm, peaceful*

trasporto *transport*

trattare *to treat, deal in/with, to negotiate, to be about*

trattato *treaty; treated*

trattoria *restaurant, country inn*

tre *three*

tredici *thirteen*

treno *train*

trenta *thirty*

triste *sad*

troppo *too much*

trovare *to find*

tu *you (informal)*

il tuo, la tua, i tuoi, le tue *your, yours*

tuonare *to thunder,* **tuono** *thunder*

turista *(m. and f.);* **turistico/a/ci/che** *tourist*

turno *turn,* **chiuso per turno** *closed by rota*

tutto *all, everything*

uccello *bird*

UE (Unione Europea) *European Union*

ufficiale *official*

ufficio *office*

ultimo/a *last, latest*

umido *humid, damp*

un, uno, una, un' *a, an, one*

undicesimo/a *eleventh*

undici *eleven*

uomo *man*

uovo *(pl.* **uova***) egg*

urbano/a *urban; local telephone call*

usare *to use*

uscire *to go/come out*

utente *user, (gas) consumer, (telephone) suscriber;* **utenza** *use*

utilizzare *to (make) use (of)*

uva *grapes*

vacanza *vacation, holiday(s), day off*

vaglia postale *postal order*

valere *to be valid, to be worth, to count, to be of use*

valido *valid*

valigia *suitcase*

valuta *currency*

vaporetto *water bus, steamboat*

variare *to vary*

vario/a/i/e *varied;* **vari(e)** *(pl.) various, several*

vaso *vase*

vecchio *old*

vedere *to see*

vedovo/a *widower, widow*

vela *sail*

veloce *fast, quick, rapid*

vendere *to sell*

venerdì *Friday*

Venezia *Venice*

venire *to come*

venti *twenty*

vento *wind*

verde *(m./f.) green*

verdura *vegetables*

vero/a *real, true, genuine*

versamento *(commerce) deposit*

vestirsi *to get dressed*

vestito *dress, suit*

vetrina *(shop) window*

via *road, street*

viaggiare *to travel*

viaggiatore/trice *traveller, passenger*

viaggio *journey, trip, voyage, (air) flight*

vicino/a *near, nearby; neighbour*

vietato *forbidden*

vigile (urbano) municipal police
vigili del fuoco fire brigade
villeggiatura holiday, vacation
vincere to win
vino wine
viola (invariable) violet, purple
violinista (m./f.) violinist
virgola comma, (maths) decimal point
vita life
vitello veal
vivanda food
vivere to live
voce (f.) voice
voglia wish, desire; **avere voglia** to
    feel like

voi you (pl.)
volere to want
**(il) vostro, (la) vostra, (i) vostri,
    (le) vostre** your(s) (pl)
volta time, **una volta** once
vuoto/a empty, vacant

zaino backpack, rucksack
zero zero, nought, nil
zio/a (pl. **zii/zie**) uncle, aunt
zona area
zucca pumpkin, (vegetable) marrow
zucchero sugar
zucchina, zucchino courgette, (Am.)
zucchini